A

CHICHESTER MISCELLANY

A CHICHESTER MISCELLANY

Copyright © Phil Hewitt, 2013

Illustrations by Claire Plimmer

All rights reserved.

No part of this book may be reproduced by any means, nor transmitted, nor translated into a machine language, without the written permission of the publishers.

Phil Hewitt has asserted his right to be identified as the author of this work in accordance with sections 77 and 78 of the Copyright, Designs and Patents Act 1988.

Summersdale Publishers Ltd
46 West Street
Chichester
West Sussex
PO19 1RP
UK

www.summersdale.com

Printed and bound by CPI Group (UK) Ltd, Croydon, CR0 4YY

ISBN: 978-1-84953-379-9

Substantial discounts on bulk quantities of Summersdale books are available to corporations, professional associations and other organisations. For details contact Nicky Douglas by telephone: +44 (0) 1243 756902, fax: +44 (0) 1243 786300 or email: nicky@ summersdale.com.

A

CHICHESTER
MISCELLANY

PHIL HEWITT

summersdale

CHICHESTER

*Few towns in England have so much to offer of
the real values which make life worth living.*
CHICHESTER CITY GUIDE, 1953

CONTENTS

Chichester People

Chichester Culture

FOREWORD

by the Duke of Richmond and Gordon

Chichester is a city with an ancient heritage, stretching back to its foundation almost two thousand years ago. Over the millennia, successive generations have left their mark on the city; a walk of just a few minutes takes us from the Roman city walls to the Norman cathedral, and on to the sixteenth-century Market Cross and the Georgian and Victorian splendours of the commercial heart of the city. Historic architecture exists side by side with modernity, most particularly in the Pallant House Gallery, whose collection of modern art is housed within a Queen Anne townhouse linked to a striking twenty-first-century extension, and The Novium, Chichester's new city museum, where visitors can view the foundations of a first-century Roman bathhouse before journeying up through the eras to look out over the chimney-pots and roof-tops of a city at once both ancient and thoroughly up to date.

My own connections to Chichester began over 300 years ago, when the 1st Duke of Richmond (I am the 10th) bought a hunting box at Goodwood. I am proud to have been involved with many aspects of Sussex life throughout my career, in institutions such as the Sussex Heritage Trust, the Chichester Cathedral Trust, the Sussex County Cricket Club and the Chichester Festivities. I think it can be fairly stated that no other city of Chichester's size offers such a unique diversity of cultural institutions, and I am delighted to see old traditions continuing and new ones being set in train, such as the redevelopment of Chichester Festival Theatre.

It is a pleasure to see the people and places of this historic city brought together in *A Chichester Miscellany* by Phil Hewitt, a collection of engaging stories covering everything from the Roman occupation and the Civil War to the city's much-loved cinemas and even its ghosts! I hope it will help to show tourists and residents alike just how much Chichester has to offer.

Richmond
March 2013

FOREWORD

by Kate Mosse

I am a Cicestrian, a resident of Chichester. Like many others who were born and raised and sent to school here, I left to spread my wings, only to return years later with a family to the folds of the Downs, the echoing cloisters of the cathedral cutting through from South Street to West Street, the green spaces of Priory Park, the secret alleyways between North Street and East Street, the Crooked 'S'. Wherever I lived, Chichester still felt like home and, as Dorothy says, 'There's no place like home...'

Everywhere one looks, there is evidence of the past. The Georgian red stone and the Roman flint, the cross at the heart of the city and the bell tower. We often walk, unseeing, through this familiar landscape, subconsciously appreciating the architecture and the asymmetry of the streets, the distinctive nooks and crannies, but not stopping to wonder how or why Chichester came to be the way it is.

This gem of a book – from Phil Hewitt, who has mapped Chichester's artistic endeavours for the past twenty years and more – reveals the secrets of our city. Within these pages, the changing face of the grand and not-so-grand streets, and the celebrated landmarks, the artists and the writers, the cathedral and the theatre. The buildings that have survived and the buildings that have been lost. A wonderful tumbling of facts and anecdotes, stories of antiquity and of the present, the coincidences and acts of bad luck – or good – history made on these cobbled streets. The famous sons and daughters, the less well-known names who nonetheless made their mark, from pre-Roman times to these headlong days of the twenty-first century.

This is Chichester from cradle to grave, a city that is itself a snapshot of our island story. A book for anyone who loves Chichester, past or present, for all of us who have made our homes here, it is a pleasure from start to finish. Best of all, it even explains the derivation of the well-worn word 'Cicestrian'...

Kate Mosse

March 2013

Welcome to Chichester

Chichester is a place rooted in its past, but confident in its future; a place which looks back with pride but forward with optimism. It is a delightful place to live, a delightful place to work and a delightful place to visit.

My first boss in the city warned me that Chichester is the 'graveyard of ambition', but in fact the description is a compliment. Come to Chichester, and you will struggle to find anywhere you would rather be.

I have worked in Chichester for twenty-two years now, and I have relished exploring the heritage of a city which is genuinely entrancing. In my time on the *Chichester Observer*, I have watched fire and floods, and literally hundreds of plays at Chichester Festival Theatre. I have seen the city fighting to protect its history and working to ensure its tomorrow. Little stays the same in our busy world, but there is a thread of Chichester that remains resolutely Chichester, and it is to this that I dedicate the book.

Across the pages that follow, I offer a broadly chronological sweep through the centuries which have left Chichester with a Roman street plan, a Norman cathedral, a beautiful market cross dating back to *c*.1500, a range of splendid Georgian buildings and a modern art gallery ranked among the very finest in the country.

But for the sake of clarity, I have arranged this miscellany so as to give four intermingling flavours of the city.

The chapters labelled **Chichester Times** look at important moments in the creation of modern-day Chichester, while those headed **Chichester Places** celebrate the buildings which give Chichester its distinctive character. The **Chichester Culture** chapters recognise the wealth of artists, musicians, actors and writers associated with the city. They also look at the artistic endeavours which make Chichester the important cultural centre it is today. The **Chichester People** chapters bring together the major figures, be they visionaries or adventurers, saints or sinners, who have played their part in the city's rich history.

Taken together, these four strands paint a vivid picture of Chichester, a city I hope you will enjoy exploring with me now.

Phil Hewitt
March 2013

A 'Satisfying' City

Few English cities are so satisfying as
Chichester, so good to look at, so nicely
planned, or, I should think, so pleasant to live
in. Lying as it does in a plain, it is endowed
with none of the striking characteristics of some
of the other cathedral cities – the commanding
position of Lincoln, the dramatic setting of
Durham or the hills that enfold Wells. But
without any of these natural advantages it
seems to me to possess nearly all the qualities
an English city should have.

ARTHUR OSWALD, *CHICHESTER CITY GUIDE*, 1953

The cathedral city of Chichester lies in the county of West Sussex on the coastal plain of the English Channel, approximately 75 miles south-west of London. The chalk hills of the South Downs lie to the north; to the south lies Chichester Harbour, connected to the city by canal. The nearest major city is Portsmouth, 18 miles to the west. Just to the east is Goodwood House, home to the Dukes of Richmond on an estate synonymous with horse racing and the best of British motor racing. The town of Arundel, seat of the Dukes of Norfolk, lies 11 miles to the east.

Chichester was recorded as *Clssaceastre* or *Cisseceastre* in 895 and *Cicestre* in the Domesday Book of 1086. It is likely that the name means 'Roman town of a chieftain called Cissa', son of Aelle, the first king of the South Saxons in the late fifth century. A *ceastra* was an Anglo Saxon fortified camp, so the name would mean 'Cissa's Camp'. However, it is possible that the first element of the name is the Old English word *cisse* meaning 'a gravelly feature'. In an era when dialects are under threat nationwide, you can still hear older Cicestrians – in a remnant of Sussex dialect – refer to the city as 'Chiddester'. Chichester is the county town of West Sussex and a city rich in Sussex history.

What the Romans Did for Chichester

In conception and design, Chichester is a Roman town, with evidence of its Roman origins still very much apparent today.

In AD 43, the Emperor **Claudius** sent **Aulus Plautius** with four legions to conquer Britain. A politician of the mid first century, he served as the first governor of the new province from AD 43 to AD 47. Following Plautius's lead, Claudius himself then led the victorious Roman army across the Thames into Essex, while on the south coast the campaigns were conducted by the future emperor **Vespasian,** who was in command of the Second Augustan Legion. Effectively it was Vespasian who founded Chichester as a Roman town. The invasion of Sussex saw relatively little bloodshed; some historians argue it was almost friendly, certainly by comparison with other parts of the country.

Close to the coast, Fishbourne was conveniently situated for seaborne supplies, and so it was here that Vespasian set up winter quarters for his men (probably in AD 43/44). Over time, the military base became a magnificent palace, built over the site of the original camp. Now a major tourist attraction, Fishbourne Roman Palace was completed by the late AD 70s.

The palace was discovered and initially excavated in the early 1960s. Some historians – though others beg to differ – believe that it was erected by **Cogidubnus** or **Togidubnus**, British king of the Regnenses (alternatively Regni or Regini), although it seems he may not have lived to see it completed.

Cogidubnus's dates are uncertain, but the consensus is that he was alive in the late first century. He remains a figure shrouded in mystery, but he would seem to have been a loyal friend to Rome. Some historians argue that he was effectively a puppet king, a man with existing local influence whose usefulness was recognised by the Romans and consequently exploited. Indeed, his forenames – Tiberius Claudius – indicate he was granted Roman citizenship. It is possible that the Romans created his kingdom and that, as part of the deal, he granted them safe haven at Fishbourne on Chichester Harbour.

The growth of nearby Chichester can be safely ascribed to Cogidubnus's influence, though it is likely that his Regnenses tribe already had some kind of settlement on the site. The Romans set about developing a new town and called it Noviomagus, a name which brings together the Celtic words for 'new' and 'field' or 'plain' in Romanised form. The name is also recorded as Noviomagus Reginorum, Regnorum, Regnentium and Regentium, names linking it to the Regnenses tribe. The town established itself along predictable Roman lines, with the usual Roman features, many of which still exist:

The **Roman Baths** were situated in the north-west quadrant of the city and would have been housed within a large public building, perhaps spanning 5,500 square metres. As was generally the case in Roman towns, the baths were a place to see and be seen, a place where business deals were done, where plots and plans were hatched and where political debate was thrashed out – a centre for all that would be described as networking today. The baths are now the centrepiece of Chichester's new district museum, the Novium, which was opened in July 2012.

The **City Walls** we see today are medieval, with much eighteenth- and nineteenth-century restoration, but they were built on Roman foundations. Originally, the walls would have been of earth and timber, constructed towards the end of the second century, very likely simply to delimit the city, as historians do not believe the city was under threat at the time. The gates that were later added to create Northgate, Southgate, Westgate and Eastgate have long since gone, but much of the walls, steeply banked on one side, flint on the other, can still be walked – a rarity in British cities. The walls are an excellent way to appreciate both the city and the way it has developed, and the twentieth century saw an increasing awareness that they must be conserved and protected. The Chichester Walls Walk Trust is active in their promotion, and The City Walls Partnership also works to ensure their preservation.

The **Roman amphitheatre** was built in the first century outside the city's south-east quadrant, on the east side of the town. All that is visible now is a depression in the grass, but the amphitheatre would have seated about 800 people, all gathered to enjoy a wide range of games. Gladiators almost certainly fought to the death in Chichester; bear-baiting was another of the spectator sports indulged. The amphitheatre was located partly next to what is now Chichester's Cattle Market car park.

The **Roman basilica** would have been the civic centre of the old Roman town. The best evidence would suggest that it is located probably somewhere under Chichester Cathedral.

Rather more visible is the **Cogidubnus Stone,** which records the erection of a temple to Minerva (location unknown). Excavated in 1723, the stone is now on the outside of the Assembly Rooms in North Street. In the stones's inscription, the first two letters of the king's native name are missing. It is usually reconstructed as 'Cogidubnus', following the majority of manuscripts of Tacitus, but some, including the distinguished archaeologist Professor Sir Barry Cunliffe of Oxford University, believe 'Togidubnus' is the more linguistically correct form.

The remains of a number of **Roman houses** have also been found within the city.

Chichester Cathedral

England can boast of many cathedrals, loftier, larger, more grandiose, and more abundant in fine detail, but few more graceful and harmonious than queenly Chichester.
CHICHESTER CITY GUIDE, 1949

Chichester Cathedral is the city's great glory. It has welcomed pilgrims and visitors for more than nine centuries. In an era when many cathedrals charge admission, the cathedral authorities in Chichester have always made it a point of principle not to do so. Architectural historian **Nikolaus Pevsner** lauded Chichester's as 'the most typical English cathedral'. The main part of the church is wholly Norman in design, but additions down the centuries chart the course of English church and cathedral architecture.

Fires and disasters have marked the history of Chichester Cathedral, not least the day the spire collapsed in February 1861, but the cathedral's progress has been one of addition rather than one of complete renewal, and in that sense, it can be said to embrace all the great periods of ecclesiastical building in this country.

The origins of Chichester Cathedral lie in Selsey. **Saint Wilfrid** (AD 634–709) – whose name lives on in the name of Chichester's hospice – brought Christianity to Sussex in AD 681 when he established a cathedral in Selsey. Four centuries later, the Normans, following their conquest of England in 1066, decided that cathedrals should be in large centres of population, rather than small towns. Consequently, in 1075 the Council of London established the See of Chichester and thereby transferred the seat of the bishop to our city. By then Chichester had been a place of increasing importance for at least a century, but the bishopric was one of the country's poorest, a fact which almost certainly explains the relative smallness of the cathedral it inspired. Thanks to the beauty of its proportions, the cathedral offers a great feeling of spaciousness as you enter, but the building itself ranks as relatively modest in size.

Building began under **Bishop Stigand** in around 1076, an important time for Norman architecture in this country. Canterbury Cathedral was at or nearing completion, and work was underway at a number of sites. Norman in design, Chichester Cathedral rose, as did so many other buildings, as an emblem of the new power in the land. In their architecture, the Normans were rugged and vigorous, a reflection of their conquering spirit, and these were qualities at the heart of Chichester Cathedral.

After the early work by Stigand, it was **Ralph de Luffa** (or Ralph Luffa), Bishop of Chichester from 1091 to 1123, who took the building through to completion in time for its dedication to the Holy Trinity in 1108. However, Luffa's job was not finished with the dedication. When the new building was badly damaged by fire in 1114, it was Bishop Luffa who ensured the cathedral was restored. Historians take the view that he was in effect the cathedral's founder and that it is his church we stand in today. He remains one of Chichester's most celebrated bishops and is commemorated in the name of one of the city's current secondary schools.

Another fire badly damaged the cathedral in 1187, but fortunately another resolute bishop was to hand. **Bishop Seffrid** determined to do his very best despite meagre resources. The fire had destroyed the wooden roof and damaged the east end of the cathedral, so stone vaulting and a new clerestory had to be built, as the cathedral moved closer to the building we know today. The cathedral was rededicated in 1199, though it would seem unlikely the repairs were complete at that time. Significant work was also carried out in the thirteenth century when the north and south porches were built and chapels were added to the nave aisles.

One of Chichester's distinctions is that it is the country's only cathedral with a detached medieval bell tower. It is 36 metres high and 11 metres square at the base, and was built when the cathedral's central tower had become too weak to carry its bells. Construction lasted from about 1375 to around 1440. At one point early on, it was known as Ryman's or Raymond's Tower – a name now lost. Extensive restoration was carried out during 1902–1908.

During the fifteenth century, the cloisters were added to the cathedral, enclosing the south transept. Heavily restored in 1890, the cloisters are now home to the cathedral's administrative offices and also its café and shop.

The prettiest thing at Chichester is a charming little three-sided cloister, attached to the cathedral, where, as is usual in such places, you may sit upon a grave stone amid the deep grass in the middle, and measure the great central mass of the church, the large gray sides, the high foundations of the spire, the parting of the nave and transept. From this point the greatness of a cathedral seems more complex and impressive. You watch the big shadows slowly change their relations; you listen to the cawing of rooks and the twittering of swallows; you hear a slow footstep echoing in the cloisters.

HENRY JAMES, *PORTRAITS OF PLACES*, 1883

Other noteworthy buildings associated with Chichester Cathedral include the Bishop's Palace, repaired and enlarged in 1725 and again in 1880, just south-west of the cathedral. On the eastern side of the cathedral, just off South Street, is the Vicars' Hall, founded towards the end of the fourteenth century and now used for talks and dinners.

As it moves towards its thousandth anniversary, Chichester Cathedral remains an important place of worship, much of it centred on the cathedral's choir, regarded among the very finest in the country. The choir's wide-ranging liturgical repertoire is at the heart of the daily offering of worship in the cathedral's warm and welcoming acoustic.

The statutes at Chichester Cathedral provide for eighteen trebles and six lay vicars in its choir. The choristers are educated at the Prebendal, the cathedral school, close by in West Street. The boys start as probationers in school year 3 or 4 (aged seven to nine), and usually become full choristers a year later. The lay vicars are professional singers and live in or near the Cathedral Close.

In addition to cathedral services, Chichester Cathedral Choir takes part in festivals, including the Southern Cathedrals Festival, which rotates between Chichester, Winchester and Salisbury each summer. At the time of writing, the 'Organist and Master of the Choristers' is Sarah Baldock.

In January 1956 **Philip Larkin** visited Chichester Cathedral and was inspired to write 'An Arundel Tomb'. The poem, published in 1964 in Larkin's collection *The Whitsun Weddings*, describes the tomb of Richard FitzAlan, 10th Earl of Arundel (*d*.1376), and his second wife, Eleanor of Lancaster (*d*.1372). It opens:

> *Side by side, their faces blurred,*
> *The earl and countess lie in stone,*

Larkin described the effigies as 'extremely affecting', particularly in the way the knight has removed his gauntlet so he can hold his wife's hand. 'What will survive of us is love,' Larkin writes, and indeed the Larkin poem can be read as a reflection on the nature of love. Arguably, it is just as striking as a reflection on the passage of time and the inevitability of death.

Chichester's Very Own Saint

Every self-respecting city should have a saint. Chichester's is **St Richard**, whose name lives on in the city's St Richard's Hospital. St Richard's other great legacy is his celebrated prayer:

> *Thanks be to thee, my Lord Jesus Christ,*
> *for all the benefits thou hast given me, for*
> *all the pains and insults which thou hast*
> *borne for me. O most merciful Redeemer,*
> *Friend and Brother, may I know thee*
> *more clearly, love thee more dearly and*
> *follow thee more nearly, day by day.*

The words are known to many on account of the Stephen Schwartz and John-Michael Tebelak musical *Godspell*, in which the words form part of the song 'Day By Day'.

St Richard was born Richard Wyche, De Wych, or De Wicio in 1197 or 1198 in Droitwich, Worcestershire. He was elected Bishop of Chichester in 1244 and consecrated by Pope Innocent IV in 1245. Richard died on 3 April 1253 in Dover.

History records that Richard lived at Tarring in the parish priest's house, visited his diocese on foot, and cultivated figs in his spare time. It also records that he was an excellent administrator and an accessible man of great spirituality, capable of both sternness and mercy towards the sinners in his diocese. Towards the end of his life, he was a great supporter of the Crusades, energetically recruiting the men of Sussex and Kent to their cause.

St Richard was canonised in 1262. His shrine in Chichester Cathedral was a focus for pilgrims until it was despoiled in 1538 under the order of Thomas Cromwell. St Richard's body was reburied secretly. Since 2007, his saint's day, 16 June, has been celebrated as Sussex Day.

At the western entrance to Chichester Cathedral stands **Philip Jackson's** statue of St Richard. Bronze and one and a half times life-size, it was commissioned by the Friends of Chichester Cathedral to celebrate the millennium and was unveiled by the Bishop of Chichester in 2000. St Richard stands, hand raised in peace, to greet visitors to the cathedral. Another of Philip Jackson's sculptures, *Christ in Judgement* (1998), can be found inside the cathedral.

Based in Midhurst, Mr Jackson is arguably the country's foremost public sculptor. His other works include *The Young Mozart* in Belgravia, London; the *Falklands War Sculpture* – known as the 'The Yomper' – outside the Royal Marines Museum, Eastney, Portsmouth; *King George VI* at the Britannia Royal Naval College, Dartmouth; the (1966) *World Cup Sculpture* in Newham, London; *Queen Elizabeth II* in Windsor Great Park; and *Bobby Moore* at the new Wembley Stadium. Mr Jackson's trademark is his ability to capture personality through body language and expression, creating both drama and presence through his meticulous posturing of the figures he depicts. His subjects range from the historical to the instantly recognisable; all are conveyed with power and beauty. Mr Jackson was appointed Commander of the Royal Victorian Order (CVO) in the Queen's 2009 Birthday Honours list.

CHICHESTER PLACES

Past Churches, Present Uses

Chichester isn't unique in its wealth of redundant city-centre churches, but certainly there is interest in the differing fates which have befallen its former church buildings, some considerably happier than others.

Fortunately the former church of **St Peter the Great** no longer languishes under the name 'The Slurping Toad' – the sad, but brief, fate which befell one of West Street's grandest Victorian buildings. Consecrated in 1852, the church was constructed in the fourteenth-century style. For more than a century, St Peter the Great served proudly as the mother church of the city, happy to be in the shadow of the cathedral, the mother church of the diocese. With time, however, its congregation diminished and, by the end of the 1970s, the church was deemed redundant. The building became a shopping arcade before becoming The Slurping Toad pub in 1997. It is now Wests bar and lounge, where diners and drinkers can relax under the coloured glow of its stained-glass windows.

The former church of **St Andrew, Oxmarket** is one of the city's most successful church transformations, thriving now as the city's Oxmarket Centre of Arts.

Tucked away off East Street, the building dates back to the thirteenth century, but wasn't used for services again after it suffered bomb damage in 1943. In 1975, it became the arts centre, establishing itself as an important showcase for local painters and makers. The poet William Collins was buried in St Andrew's churchyard in 1759, but the graveyard has now gone.

Also enjoying a new lease of life in the arts world is the former **St John's Chapel**, an important venue for talks and musical events during the summer months. The chapel was built at a time when the population of

the city's south-east quadrant was expanding rapidly, and it was funded in the most modern of ways. Share issues paid for its construction in 1812; the sale or rent of private pews paid for its running. But numbers fell away. St John's was amalgamated with nearby St Pancras where the congregations eventually converged. St John's was closed in 1973, and remained so for nearly twenty years until its revival in 1992. It is now in the care of the Churches Conservation Trust.

Rather less public now is the former **All Saints in the Pallant**, tucked away off South Street. Built in the first half of the thirteenth century, it was deconsecrated after World War Two and served for many years as a British Red Cross centre. It is now an office. But at least it is still there, unlike St Peter the Less.

St Peter the Less lived up to its name when it was bulldozed in 1960 in one of the more shameful moments of Chichester's post-war redevelopment.

Standing in North Street, it was the largest of Chichester's medieval churches. Nonetheless, it was auctioned off for just £3,000 and subsequently flattened. Possibly Saxon in origin, it definitely dated back to at least the middle of the thirteenth century. Part of the site is now a road named St Peter's.

Another ancient Chichester church lost to posterity was **St Martin's,** which stood in St Martin's Street. Probably built in the tenth century, it was demolished in 1906. A public garden – a little oasis of calm – now respectfully marks a spot which saw nine centuries of worship. A plaque by the garden gate advises 'Service for the united parishes now held in the Church of St Olave', but just like the church, the plaque was overtaken by events.

St Olave's Church in North Street is the only one of Chichester's former churches to retain a religious purpose. Built around 1050, it is the oldest building in Chichester. Taking its name from St Olave or Olaf, King Olaf Haraldsson, Patron Saint of Norway, the church contains evidence of late eleventh century work, but was partly rebuilt in the late thirteenth and early fourteenth centuries. The Victorian era brought further restoration and a link with the doomed St Martin's nearby. Sadly, like St Martin's, St Olave's could not withstand the effects of dwindling city-centre congregations. The building became the city's SPCK bookshop in 1958. Founded in 1698, the Society for Promoting Christian Knowledge aims to help people grow in the Christian faith.

With all these churches now gone, **Chichester Cathedral** in West Street is the only truly city-centre place of worship. Most of Chichester's currently active churches are close to the city walls or just outside. They include: Chichester Baptist Church, Sherborne Road; Christchurch Methodist and United Reformed Church, Old Market Avenue; St Paul's Church, Churchside; Revelation Church, Spur Road; St Wilfrid's Church, Sherborne Road; St Richard's Church, Cawley Road; St Pancras Church, St Pancras; and St George's Church, Cleveland Road.

CHICHESTER CULTURE

Chichester Musicians

Chichester is a city which prides itself on the wealth and breadth of its culture. For centuries, music has been central to the creative life of the city. Many musicians and composers have enjoyed strong associations with Chichester.

One of Chichester's bad boys, **Thomas Weelkes** (*c.*1575–1623) was appointed organist of Chichester Cathedral in around 1601. Not exactly assiduous in attending services, he became known for his outrageous behaviour and heavy drinking. There are even reports that he once urinated on the Dean from the organ loft during Evensong. Weelkes was famously dismissed by the cathedral authorities for drunkenness and profanity in 1617. In later life, he appears to have had a stormy relationship with authority in general, but Weelkes remains one of his era's most prolific and important composers of madrigals. Nearly a hundred of them survive. He is still regarded as a significant figure, not least in Chichester where the Cathedral Choir will generally sing as many as five pieces by Weelkes per term.

Theodore Aylward is believed to have been born in Chichester in around 1730. He died in London on 27 February 1801. An organist and composer, he was one of the assistant directors at the Handel Commemoration of 1784. In his day, he was a noted composer for the theatre.

English organist, theorist and composer **John Keeble** was born in Chichester in about 1711 and died in London on 24 December 1786. A former choirboy at Chichester Cathedral, he is remembered for his *Select Pieces for the Organ* (1777–*c*.1780). His theoretical work *The Theory of Harmonics, or an Illustration of the Grecian Harmonics* was published in 1784.

John Marsh, who died in Chichester in 1828, wrote the only surviving English symphonies from the late eighteenth century. Born in 1752, he moved to Chichester in 1787 where he directed subscription concerts and sometimes stood in for the cathedral organist. It was largely thanks to his presence that Chichester enjoyed a lively concert life at this time. Marsh lived in North Pallant, Chichester for the last forty years of his life. He was also active in the anti-slavery movement. Of great interest now is Marsh's *History of My Private Life*, journals which he kept from 1765. Now held in the Huntington Library, San Marino, California, they run to 6,704 pages – a vivid account of life in the Chichester area at that time. Despite efforts to keep them in this country, the journals were sold into the States by Christie's in 1991.

The ashes of **Gustav Holst** (1874–1934) are buried in Chichester Cathedral, in memory of the Whitsun Festivals he directed there and also his friendship with Chichester's celebrated wartime bishop, George Bell, who described Holst as 'a prince of friends'. Holst's best-known composition is his orchestral work *The Planets*, which remains enduringly popular, although he also composed over two hundred other works including ballets, songs and operas.

Norman Demuth, a celebrated young English composer at the time and later Professor of Composition at the Royal Academy of Music, took over as conductor of the Chichester Orchestral Society from 1929 until 1935. The Society is now the Chichester Symphony Orchestra. Born in 1898, Demuth died in Chichester on 21 April 1968. His works include *Threnody for Strings* and *Overture for a Joyful Occasion*.

Eric Coates, who died in the Royal West Sussex Hospital, Chichester, on 21 December 1957, is perhaps best known for the 'Dambusters March' (1954) and also for 'By the Sleepy Lagoon' (1930), which is still used to introduce the long-running radio programme *Desert Island Discs*. Coates enjoyed a long association with the nearby village of Selsey dating back to 1922. He and his wife lived at various times in six different houses in Selsey, one in Sidlesham and one in Bognor Regis, remaining in the area – barring the war years – until Coates's death in Chichester at the age of seventy-one, following a stroke.

English contralto **Gladys Ripley**, who was born in Essex in 1908, was a popular performer in opera, oratorio, musical plays and light music. She worked with the leading orchestras of her day under big-name conductors including Adrian Boult, Malcolm Sargent, Thomas Beecham and Wilhelm Furtwängler. During World War Two, she sang for the troops in

France, West Africa, Belgium and the Netherlands. In 1954, her third marriage brought her to Chichester where she died the following year, aged 47.

English conductor and teacher **Paul Steinitz**, who was born in Chichester on 25 August 1909, was an important figure in twentieth-century interpretation of the music of Johann Sebastian Bach. Steinitz founded the London Bach Society and Steinitz Bach Players. He died in Old Oxted, Surrey, on 21 April 1988.

Leonard Bernstein's significance for Chichester lies in the *Chichester Psalms*, which he composed for Chichester Cathedral. A setting of a Hebrew text for countertenor, chorus and orchestra, it was performed in the cathedral in July 1965. Bernstein, whose works range from symphonies to popular musicals, was born on 25 August 1918 in Massachusetts and died on 14 October 1990 in New York.

Singer **Petula Clark** enjoys strong family connections with Chichester where her parents lived in Priory Road. Born in 1932, Clark is one of the country's most successful female recording artists. She also became America's number one female vocalist during the British musical invasion of the 1960s. Along with The Beatles, Clark conquered the international world of pop with hits including 'Downtown', which earnt her the first of two American Grammies. A string of classics followed, including 'This Is My Song', 'I Know a Place', 'My Love', 'I Couldn't Live Without Your Love', 'Don't Sleep in the Subway', 'Colour My World' and 'The Other Man's Grass Is Always Greener'.

Scottish tenor saxophonist **Bobby Wellins** (*b*.1936) taught in the jazz department at the West Sussex Institute of Higher Education in Chichester and has long lived in the area. Wellins's most important work was with Stan Tracey in The New Departures Quartet. He was a key figure in Tracey's recording

Under Milk Wood in 1965, a collection of themes inspired by Dylan Thomas's play.

American composer, organist and pianist **William Albright** (1944–1998) wrote the *Chichester Mass* (1974), commissioned for the 900th anniversary in 1975 of the establishment of the See of Chichester.

Chichester-born musicologist **Richard Toop** (*b.*1945) is an important figure in Australia where he has lived for many years. His reputation lies in his teaching of composers and his lectures. His publications have focused on late twentieth-century music, particularly Stockhausen.

CHICHESTER PLACES

Market Cross

Chichester Cathedral stands as the enduring symbol of the city's heavenly aspirations. The city's **Market Cross** is the great symbol of its earthbound success – a daily reminder that, after the decline of the Romans, Chichester continued to thrive on the back of its trading strength.

Medieval Chichester saw a wealth of different trades and industries flourish in the city. Leathermaking was concentrated in the Pallants in the south-east quadrant of the city centre; needlemaking was the dominant business just outside the city walls to the east; and Chichester's wool staple – its right to trade in wool – was established in 1314. Chichester became a significant exporter of wool, and by the fourteenth century there were many cloth workers living in the city. Two current street names – Needlemakers and The Woolstaplers – reflect this past.

More important still was the city's trade in livestock, which continued in the city centre until the nineteenth century. For hundreds of years, sheep, cows, horses, bullocks, donkeys and goats were sold in East Street, calves in North Street, and sheep and pigs up to Northgate. The tradition ended when the late Victorians decided that enough was enough. The streets were left in an appalling state after the animals had left, and the health of the city was poor as a result.

From the Middle Ages, Chichester was also an important centre in the wine trade. In the 1300s wine was imported in exchange for Chichester wool, and wine remained a significant part of the city's commerce for many centuries to come. Indeed, it was for the wine merchant Henry Peckham that Pallant House – now a major art gallery – was built in 1712 in the city's south-east quadrant. Also important was the corn trade, a reflection of the city's significance as a grain-growing area. In the 1830s, Chichester became one of the first cities in Britain to build a Corn Exchange. Later a cinema, the building in East Street is now the clothes shop Next.

Chichester's Market Cross is the legacy of the city's trading heritage. Standing at the intersection of the Roman roads which run north-south and east-west through the city, it was given to the city by Edward Story (or Storey), who served as Bishop of Chichester from 1478 until his death in 1503. The idea was to provide somewhere for the poor to sell their wares – a role it carried out until the Butter Market was opened in North Street in 1808 when trading at the cross ceased.

The cross now stands as an architectural gem, a key gathering point in moments of national crisis and celebration. Built of Caen stone, it comprises eight sides around a central shaft on which sits a cupola, supported by eight flying buttresses. Internally, the ribbed vaulting springs from the massive central shaft to small pillars at the outer wall. Important renovations and restorations were carried out in 1746 and in 1930.

The east side of the Cross contains a bust of Charles I, added by Charles II in posthumous tribute to his father. Charles I now looks out at a city which played a part in his execution. The current bust is a facsimile of the original which is now housed in Chichester's Pallant House Gallery. The original is generally believed to be by Hubert Le Sueur (*c*.1590–*c*.1658) and was created in gilded bronze in around 1637, some years before its subject's death in 1649.

The Civil War Brings Desecration

The English Civil War brought devastation to Chichester in a grim chapter in the city's history.

At the outbreak of war, the local gentry and clergy generally supported the Royalists while the citizens and merchants, including Chichester MP **William Cawley**, mostly supported Parliament. In November 1642, a party of Royalists turned up and claimed Chichester for the King. Cawley promptly alerted Parliament, and General **Sir William Waller** was despatched to Sussex to retake the city.

Waller took up position on the raised ground of the Broyle, ancient earthworks just to the north of the city centre. He set up his artillery, and when the cannon fell short, he moved his men round to just outside Westgate. He also attacked from the

WILLIAM CAWLEY

east. During the siege, both Westgate and Eastgate suffered considerable damage, much of it self-inflicted by the defenders who burnt down houses in an attempt to deny cover to the invading forces. In the end, the Royalists admitted defeat and surrendered. 'It hath pleased God to deliver Chichester into my hands after eight days siege thereof', wrote Waller. He entered the city on 29 December: his reputation as a 'William the Conqueror' was established.

Waller announced: 'Our great Care and desire was and is to preserve the Cyttie of Chichester from utter ruine', words which counted for nothing. Encouraged by Sir Arthur Hesilrige (or Haselrig), Waller's second in command, Parliamentarian troops unleashed their fury on the cathedral, defiling everything within reach in a determined orgy of desecration. They ripped up books; they destroyed fixtures and fittings; and they defaced the monuments.

While the cathedral revived with time, Chichester's needlemaking industry did not. The industry had developed in St Pancras, just outside Eastgate – precisely the area razed to the ground by attackers and defenders alike. The needleworkers' cottages were destroyed. Other casualties were two Eastgate inns, The Lion and The Dolphin, and a church in Eastgate Square which was partially destroyed. The present St Pancras Church, built in 1750–1751, stands on the site of the earlier building.

Curiously, Waller was not against the monarchy: 'I was borne under a monarchy; and I desire to dy under it', he wrote. It was left to Chichester's very own William Cawley to help ensure that Charles I was put to death – an act which means that the word 'regicide' will forever accompany Cawley's name.

Baptised in 1602, Cawley was the eldest son of Chichester brewer and three-times mayor John Cawley. After his father's death, Cawley established an almshouse for aged tradesmen in Chichester in 1626. Two years later, he gained one of the town's seats in parliament. An energetic parliamentarian and activist, Cawley was one of the members of the High Court of Justice appointed to try the King for treason in 1649. With typical enthusiasm, he attended every session of court before signing his King's death warrant. Cawley was the thirty-fifth of the fifty-nine signatories, many of whom were executed or imprisoned after the Restoration of King Charles II in 1660. Cawley, however, fled abroad and died in Switzerland in 1667.

William Juxon, Bishop of London, who became Archbishop of Canterbury in 1660, was the only priest to minister to King Charles I on the scaffold. Juxon is believed to have been born in Chichester in 1582 and attended the Prebendal, the Chichester Cathedral school. He died on 4 June 1663 in London.

Celebrate Guy Fawkes Night – or Bonfire Night, as it is more commonly called these days – and you are celebrating a tradition which Chichester helped establish. **Lancelot Andrewes** (1555–1626) was consecrated Bishop of Chichester in 1605. Following the discovery of the failed Gunpowder Plot that same year, Andrewes argued that the nation's and the church's deliverance by God should be celebrated annually – a custom still observed every year on 5 November.

Chichester's Eighteenth-century Flourish

The late seventeenth century, and the Georgian era which dominated the eighteenth century, brought a period of marked prosperity to the city of Chichester – a prosperity which reflected the thriving trades to which the city was home. Not only could you get anything you needed in Chichester, the chances were that it was actually made in Chichester, as a glance at *Bailey's British Directory* for 1784 will show. It lists a remarkable number of traders and craftsmen in the city engaged in myriad professions, many of which have long since disappeared. Here are a few of the trades recorded. While some are familiar to twenty-first-century readers, others now seem archaic and even slightly bizarre.

*Surveyor; patten maker; maltster; chemist
& druggist; corn merchant & proprietor of
the salt works; whitesmith & ironmonger;
cooper; draper; woolstapler; cordwainer;
chinaman & postmaster; saddler & harness
maker; fellmonger & glover; hatter; grocer,
chandler & soap boiler; tanner; cork cutter;
brazier & wine merchant; Comptroller of the
Customs; currier & leather cutter; mercer &
haberdasher; wine cooper; grazier; mealman
& seedsman; upholder & auctioneer; collar
maker; cabinet maker; shoe maker; breeches
maker & glover; cutler & silversmith; coach
maker; grocer & turner.*

On the back of such thriving commerce, Chichester gained many of its finest buildings. It was a time which shaped much of the city's present-day character.

Edes House in West Street predates the Georgian splendours which followed during the years of Chichester's great eighteenth-century flourish. The earliest important house in Chichester to be built in brick rather than timber, Edes House belongs architecturally to the Later Stuart period. It was built for John and Hannah Edes who married in 1693. It was probably around the time of the wedding that John began to plan a residence which befitted his status, but he died a year before its completion in 1696. For a long time, the house remained nameless but was then successively Westgate House, West Street House, Wren's House and Wren House before – acknowledging that Sir Christopher Wren almost certainly had nothing whatsoever to do with it – West Sussex County Council renamed the building Edes House in 1993.

West Sussex County Council had bought the property in 1916 and used it as council offices until

1936 when the present County Hall was built just behind Edes House. The building was subsequently used as County Library headquarters until 1967 and then as the County and Diocesan Record Offices until 1989, when the records were moved into new buildings nearby. Edes House is now used for various functions, including talks and civil ceremonies.

Many of the other houses in West Street date from the eighteenth century, a time which saw this particular street act as a magnet to the wealthy professional classes whose prosperity left its stamp on Georgian Chichester.

Pallant House in North Pallant stands to this day as a magnificent example of a Queen Anne townhouse, a product of the city's opulence in the early years of the eighteenth century. Known in its early days as Dodo House because of the poor attempt at carving ostriches on the gateposts, the house stands on the east side of North Pallant at the junction of the four Pallants, an intersection which mirrors the city's principal intersection at the Market Cross. It was built in 1712 for Henry and Elizabeth Peckham as a residence befitting a prosperous merchant. It offers a picture of symmetry with elaborate Corinthian columns flanking the imposing doorway.

From 1919, Pallant House was used as a council office, but in 1982 it embarked on a much more interesting chapter in its history, opening as an art gallery. Walter Hussey, the former Dean of Chichester Cathedral, had left his personal collection to Chichester in 1977, stipulating that it should be shown in the city. After restoration, Pallant House proved the ideal platform, a place where historic house and modern art gallery met in harmony. With success, ambitions grew; the former council annexe next door was demolished, and in 2006 Pallant House gained an award-winning contemporary wing, designed by Long & Kentish architects in association with Colin St John Wilson.

Chichester played its part in the development of vine-growing in this country. **Clement Hoare** (*c.*1788–1849) cultivated a vineyard at Sidlesham and wrote several works on the subject. The most important was *A Descriptive Account of an Improved Method of Planting and Managing the Roots of Grape Vines* (1844).

Entering the Georgian era, another key addition to the Chichester cityscape was the **theatre** in South Street. Now an Italian restaurant, it still offers the spaciousness you would associate with its original purpose, plus the attraction of a fine facade, marred, some would say, by the restaurant's considerably more modern entrance. Replacing an existing theatre on the same site, the current building opened in 1791 as part of a circuit which included Southampton, Winchester, Portsmouth and Newport on the Isle of Wight. The theatre closed in 1850, and the building was sold at auction. At various times since, it has been a brewhouse, a gymnasium, a library and a box office for Chichester Festival Theatre. The Theatres Trust comments: 'Although nothing of the theatre remains internally, the shell and roof are original, making it a rare and important example of a small, late-eighteenth-century theatre.' (www.theatrestrust.org.uk).

North Street was always the city's administrative centre, and it was here that the Georgians constructed Chichester's new **Council House**, replacing an earlier timber-framed structure. Paid for by public subscription during the mayoralty of the Duke of Richmond, it was built in 1731 in the Palladian style, though the Council House is now in effect a group of connected buildings, the most recent dating from 1881. At the top of the facade is a Latin inscription which translates as: 'In order that the council and the people of Chichester and their posterity might be happy and fortunate, this council house was begun and completed in the year of our Lord 1731, in the reign of George II, Elector And King.' The building houses the city's Assembly Room, which was an important part of the social whirl of Georgian Chichester. The great Paganini performed in the Assembly Room in 1832, and Liszt followed suit in 1840. He is said to have 'elicited the most rapturous applause'.

Another product of Georgian affluence is Chichester's **Butter Market**, which was opened in North Street in 1808 as the new home for the traders who used to operate from the Market Cross a few yards away. The facade has five openings between Roman Doric columns carrying an entablature and balustrading, above which is the coat of arms of the city. Many Cicestrians remember it as the best place to buy their droopy-goth outfits during their teenage years in the 1980s, and for a while in the late twentieth century an air of neglect hung over the building, but recent times have seen the realisation of a dream to return it to popular perceptions of Georgian elegance. The Butter Market has been relaunched as a top-end shopping experience, promising 'distinguished brands and luxury goods'. The city's Georgian forefathers would doubtless approve.

Just as West Street was predominantly residential and North Street administrative, East Street was always the city's most populous trading area, and it was here that Chichester gained another of its Georgian landmarks. The **Corn Exchange** was built in about 1830 on the southern side of East Street, adjoining Baffin's Lane. It was designed by a local architect named George Draper and funded by Chichester businessmen who became shareholders. Offering a fine example of the Greek Revivalist school, its whole point was that it should be impressive and so attract trade from neighbouring towns. The street frontage offers a pediment carried on six Greek Doric columns thrown forward over the pavement to form a covered entrance area. Such grandeur probably wasn't completely wasted during the building's years as a cinema in the first half of the twentieth century, but the building's time as a fast-food outlet ill-fitted so splendid a building. It is currently a clothes shop.

Just outside Chichester to the east is **Goodwood House**, another of the great Chichester district landmarks to flourish during the Georgian era. Built during the reign of James I, the house began life essentially as a gentleman's hunting lodge, but in 1697 it entered a much grander phase in its history when it was bought by the 1st Duke of Richmond. Under successive Dukes, the building was developed considerably throughout the eighteenth century. The original 'old house' remains at the back of the building we now see. The Palladian-style south wing was added in Portland stone between 1747 and 1750, and the great Regency state apartments were added from 1800. Recent refurbishments by the current Earl and Countess of March & Kinrara, heirs to the estate, have restored and reinforced the Regency feel.

The pugilist **Thomas Winter** (1795–1851), known as 'Tom Spring', once fought at **Birdham Bridge**, near Chichester. The crowd is said to have been 20,000 strong; the stakes were 500 guineas a side; and Spring emerged triumphant.

CHICHESTER PEOPLE

Trials and Tribulations

The moral is: no matter how tortured your genius, watch what you say to a soldier. Unwise words brought **William Blake**, engraver, artist, poet and visionary, before the law in Chichester. Blake (1757–1827) was staying in a cottage at Felpham, near Bognor Regis, at the time and was already planning to leave when, on 12 August 1803, John Scolfield, a private soldier in the 1st Regiment of Dragoons, entered the garden. Blake told him to leave. Scolfield declined, and tempers flared. Blake later confessed he took him 'by the Elbows' and 'pushed him forwards down the road', but the argument spilt over into a further confrontation at The Fox Inn. Three days later, Scolfield accused Blake of seditious expressions favouring the French and damning the king of England. Blake hotly denied it, but the matter was sent for trial on 11 January 1804 in the Chichester Guildhall, home to the County Court of Quarter Sessions. The case was dismissed, but only at the expense of a great deal of anguish on the part of the man who wrote 'And did those feet in ancient time, walk upon England's mountains green'.

Sir Travers Humphreys (1867–1956) was one of the great legal figures of the twentieth century, a man involved in some of the nation's most notorious cases. Humphreys was junior counsel in the prosecution of Hawley Harvey Crippen in 1910; he was part of the prosecution team which brought 'Brides in the Bath Murderer' George Joseph Smith to justice in 1915; and a year later, he was one of the prosecution team at Sir Roger Casement's trial for treason. From 1921 to 1926, he served as recorder of Chichester, during which time he served as junior to the Solicitor General in the prosecution of Frederick Bywaters and Edith Thompson in 1922 – a case now widely believed to be one of the country's worst miscarriages of justice. Thompson's innocence has been strongly argued ever since, as indeed has Crippen's in more recent years. At the age of eighty-two, Humphreys was also the judge at the trial of the 'Acid Bath Murderer' John George Haigh at the Lewes assizes. Haigh pleaded insanity, but was found guilty of murder and executed on 10 August 1949 at London's Wandsworth Prison.

The world of sex and drugs and rock 'n' roll came face to face with the 'Establishment' in 1967 when Chichester Crown Court became the focus of worldwide attention. And where did *The Times* stand? It came out in favour of Rolling Stones frontman **Mick Jagger** and guitarist **Keith Richards**. Wealthy rock star Richards had bought a country retreat, Redlands at West Wittering, away from the bright lights of the capital. But following a tip-off from the *News of the World*, Redlands was raided on Sunday, 12 February 1967. Drugs were found, and Jagger and Richards stood trial in Chichester. On 31 July Jagger was ordered to spend three months in prison for possession of four amphetamine tablets; Richards was sentenced to a year after being found guilty of allowing cannabis to be smoked on his property. After a night behind bars, they were released on bail the next day pending appeal – which is when *The Times* brought its influence to bear. In a celebrated editorial, the editor William Rees-Mogg asked 'Who breaks a butterfly on a wheel?' He argued the two Stones had been treated with such severity because of their celebrity. Richards's conviction was eventually overturned, and Jagger's sentence was reduced to a conditional discharge. The Stones were free to roll again.

Chichester Artists

An attractive city, an alluring coastline and the nearby splendours of the South Downs have long proved an enticing combination for artists and makers, another part of Chichester's rich cultural life. The city has long been home – temporary or permanent – to a wealth of artists, both major and minor.

Flemish painter **Jacob Huysmans** (*c.*1630–1696) lived for many years in London, but briefly retreated to Chichester after the Great Fire of London, a time when known foreigners in the capital were frequently subjected to threats and abuse.

George Smith (*c.*1713–1776) was a portrait painter who was encouraged to become a landscape painter by the 2nd and 3rd Dukes of Richmond. Ducal patronage also benefitted George's brothers William (*c.*1707–1764) and John (*c.*1717–1764), who were also noted Chichester artists. Together they were known as 'the Smiths of Chichester'. George was the middle brother and is generally regarded as the most talented of the three. His reputation rests upon his pastoral depiction of the scenery of Sussex and other parts of England. **John Smith**, the younger brother, was also a landscape painter. The two frequently worked together on the same canvas. The oldest of the three Smith brothers, **William Smith**, is believed to have been born in Guildford. He started out as a portrait painter, working in London, Gloucester and then London again before retiring to Chichester in poor health. All three brothers were buried in Chichester at the Litton cemetery, St Pancras.

Landscape painter **Abraham Pether** was born in Chichester in 1756. By the age of nine, he was playing the organ in one of the city's churches. However, art was his true calling, and the young Pether studied under fellow Cicestrian George Smith. Pether's reputation rests principally upon his depiction of moonlight subjects – a predilection which brought him the nickname 'Moonlight Pether'. *An Iron Foundry by Moonlight* and *Ship on Fire in a Gale at Night* are two typical works. Sadly he was never able to make ends meet and died in poverty in Southampton on 13 April 1812, leaving his wife and nine children destitute.

Chichester cannot claim **Joseph Mallord William Turner** (1775–1851) as its own, but the city certainly attracted him, as did the nearby estate at Petworth. In 1828 the Earl of Egremont commissioned Turner to paint four decorative panels for the dining room at Petworth House. These comprised two views of the park at Petworth, as well as a view of Chichester Canal and another of the Brighton Chain Pier.

Best known for his depictions of the heroes of the Napoleonic wars, **William Haines** (1778–1848) was an engraver and painter born in Bedhampton, near Havant in Hampshire. He was still a child when the family moved to Chichester. Haines studied at Midhurst Grammar School before travelling widely to destinations including the Cape of Good Hope and Philadelphia. He returned to England in 1805 to live in London where he specialised in miniature painting. Haines exhibited at the Royal Academy as a painter of miniatures from 1808 to 1830.

Landscape painter **Joseph Francis Gilbert** (1792–1855) lived for many years in Chichester. He is known for his celebrations of the scenery of Sussex, although he also took inspiration from other parts of the UK including Wales and the Lake District. The 5th Duke of Richmond was a patron, and consequently Gilbert painted a number of horse-racing scenes at Goodwood Racecourse.

William Joy (1803–*c*.1859) was a marine painter, as was his younger brother, **John Cantiloe Joy** (1806–1859). A contemporary noted that 'they greatly excelled in depicting water in motion, they put their vessels well upon it and were accurate in the display of sails and rigging'. Known as 'the brothers Joy' in the nineteenth-century art world, they spent their later years working in Chichester.

Wood engraver and colour printer **Alfred Reynolds** was born on 1 April 1818 at Donnington, near Chichester. He attended a school in the city's Southgate, before being apprenticed to a colour printer in Clerkenwell, London. Reynolds died in 1891.

James Charles (1851–1906) was a Lancashire-born landscape and genre painter. In 1889, he moved to Colnor House, Bosham, just to the west of Chichester. He is buried in Fulham Cemetery in London. His work was lauded for its naturalness and sunlit charm.

The English architect, writer and artist **E. S. Prior**, instrumental in establishing the Arts and Crafts Movement, died in Chichester on 19 August 1932. Born in 1852, he was a founder member of the Art Workers Guild in 1884. Other more celebrated figures associated with the Arts and Crafts Movement included William Morris (1834–1896), John Ruskin (1819–1900) and Augustus Pugin (1812–1852).

Sculptor, letter-cutter, typographic designer, calligrapher, engraver, essayist, polemicist, writer and teacher, **Eric Gill** (1882–1940) was a man of remarkable energy. Gill was born in Brighton, but in 1897 the Gill family moved to 2 North Walls, Chichester. The young Eric studied at Chichester

Technical and Art School from 1897 to 1900, and for him, Chichester became the very model of the ideal city. It was in Chichester that he developed an interest in lettering, and the Anglo-Saxon and Norman stone carvings in Chichester Cathedral proved a constant source of fascination. Gill stated his ambition was 'to make a cell of good living in the chaos of our world'. Among his many distinctions, Gill carved the Stations of the Cross for Westminster Cathedral (1914–1918). He was made an Associate of the Royal Academy in 1937 and of the Royal Society of British Sculptors in 1938. Gill's books include *Christianity and Art* (1927), *Work and Property* (1937) and *Autobiography* (1940).

John Piper's tapestry for the high altar is one of the modern-art glories of Chichester Cathedral. Piper (1903–1992) was an English painter, printmaker, stage designer and writer. He designed the 'Tapestry of the Trinity' for the cathedral in 1966.

Poet and art collector **Edward James** (1907–1984) was a man of life-affirming passions. For West Sussex, his legacy is the estate a few miles north of Chichester which was once his and is now West Dean College. In 1964, James conveyed his family mansion, art collection and estate to the Edward James Foundation, a charitable educational trust, effectively laying the groundwork for his vision to become reality: a community where the estate supports a college dedicated to the arts and crafts. In 1971, the estate opened its doors as West Dean College.

English architect and designer **Sir Hugh Casson** (1910–1999) worked on the surrealist transformation of Monkton House (1936–1938), home of Edward James at West Dean. Monkton House had been built for James's parents by Sir Edwin Lutyens, but James remodelled and redecorated it on the back of a collection that included a sofa to which Salvador Dalí gave the form and colour of Mae West's lips.

Victorian Decline

'Getting the chichesters'

Life continued into the Victorian era, with the emphasis still very much on the individual maker in a thriving market town. Some merchants and makers had two or three trades; the vast majority just the one. *Pigot and Co's Royal National And Commercial Directory* for 1839 includes the following tradesmen in the city:

Tea dealer; umbrella maker; edge-tool maker; straw hat maker; chair maker; slopseller; tallow chandler; perfumer; working cutler; staymaker; organ builder; gunsmith; watch & clockmaker; pilot; salt dealer; carver & guilder; smith; millwright; bookbinder; stone mason; barometer maker; wheelwright; woollen draper; nurseryman & seedsman.

However, in many ways, and increasingly as time passed, the Victorian years were a difficult period for Chichester, a time when poor sanitation and weekly city-centre animal markets made it a distinctly unsavoury place to be. A rapid increase in population in the first half of the nineteenth century taxed the city's meagre services to the limit. Water supply was poor, and the citizens treated the River Lavant as an open sewer. Mortality rates were high – not surprising given the awful state the central streets were left in by the cattle markets.

To his dismay, **William Henry Hudson** caught the flavour of the city in 1900:

> *Chichester is not in itself sacred, nor pleasant, nor fragrant to the nostrils. On the contrary, I am here always conscious of an odour not easily described. Perhaps it comes nearest in character to an effluvium ascending in warm*

and damp weather from the long-covered old forgotten cesspools, mixed with something more subtle or volatile like a fragrance that has lost its pleasantness. It may be musk, with which the town dames perfumed themselves in bygone centuries, still clinging to the old spot, and it may be ghost old incense, which filled the sacred buildings every day for ages before its ceremonial use was discontinued.

This odour, or this mixture of smells, of which the natives are not conscious, and the sights which meet the eye, have in my case a profoundly depressing effect. This depression is probably the malady commonly known as 'the chichesters', from which many persons who visit this town are said to suffer.

W. H. Hudson, *Nature in Downland*, 1900

Eventually, the city's stinking cattle market moved out of the city centre to open land just outside Eastgate. Animal markets continued there until 1990 on a site which is now the Cattle Market car park. But otherwise in Victorian Chichester, proposed improvements met with resistance. Mains drainage became the focus of fierce political debate in a city far from convinced of the advantages it would bring. The century was almost over by the time a proper system of drainage was installed in 1896.

Born in Chichester, **Edward Bradford Titchener** (1867–1927) was a major figure in the establishment of experimental psychology in the United States.

The day the cathedral spire collapsed

The tower and spire had been a source of continual anxiety to the Cathedral authorities for a long time.
CHICHESTER CITY GUIDE, 1915

Few things in Chichester look more permanent
or solid than the cathedral, an immense presence
in the city for more than nine centuries. However,
on a dark day in February 1861, Chichester paid a
high price for years of neglect. The cathedral was a
disaster waiting to happen – and happen it did.

By the late 1850s, the stone piers which supported
the central tower and spire were crumbling and in

a dangerous condition. By November 1860, huge cracks were appearing in the crossing piers of the cathedral – cracks big enough to put your arm in. Restoration was attempted, with workmen doing their best to shore up the piers. Timber jackets with iron hoops were used, and men worked frantically into the night as crushed mortar poured from the fissures. Ironically, vibrations from the attempted rescue work were possibly a factor in the deterioration which followed, but it was a violent electrical storm which proved the final straw. Disaster struck on Thursday, 21 February 1861.

On Thursday morning, the upper part of the pier was found cracked and audibly cracking in many directions, flaked stones fell from it, whole stones burst out and fell. Finally at half past one, the whole gave way.

R. WILLIS, *THE ARCHITECTURAL HISTORY OF CHICHESTER CATHEDRAL (AND OF BOXGROVE PRIORY AND SHOREHAM COLLEGIATE CHURCH), CHICHESTER*, 1861

Willis noted that the spire and tower telescoped down into the cathedral 'as one telescope tube slides into another', the whole fall 'being an affair of a few seconds' and doing as little damage as possible in the circumstances. Nearly all the residents in the vicinity were watching outside. Fortunately, the workmen were at lunch; no one was inside at the time, and no one was hurt.

More than £53,000 was subsequently raised to return the cathedral to a glory which had crashed down in a matter of moments. The spire was rebuilt by Sir Gilbert Scott on the original lines; and the work was completed on 28 June 1866.

Sad Ends

Fate deals the cruellest hands, and Chichester certainly hasn't been exempt.

For all his fine works in parliament, Chichester MP **William Huskisson** (1770–1830) found his true place in history as this country's first fatality of the railway age – run over by Stephenson's *Rocket*, no less.

Huskisson was elected MP for Chichester in 1812, was keenly interested in financial matters and spoke vigorously in favour of the Corn Laws as an important protection for Britain's farmers. In April 1823 he was appointed President of the Board of

Trade, and the same year became MP for Liverpool. Seven years later, he met his sad fate.

Huskisson was invited by the directors of the Liverpool and Manchester Railway to attend the line's official opening on 15 September 1830. He travelled down the line on the same train as the Duke of Wellington. When the train stopped to take on water, halfway between Manchester and Liverpool, Huskisson unwisely alighted and went to speak to the Duke who was travelling in a different carriage. Huskisson failed to notice the *Rocket* approaching on the adjacent track. When he did so, he tried to climb into the Duke's carriage but succeeded only in slipping onto the line in front of the oncoming train. His leg badly mangled, he bled profusely and died later that day.

A huge wreath from Adolf Hitler probably isn't what you would want at your funeral, but it was **Dick Seaman**'s fate to become a Nazi hero in death.

Seaman was born at Aldingbourne House, Chichester, on 4 February 1913 and learned to drive without his parents' knowledge. He later opted out of Cambridge to pursue his real love – fast cars.

Seaman's first British victory came in 1934; but it was the 1938 German Grand Prix at the Nürburgring that was his major triumph. Apparently, Seaman gave a Hitler salute on the podium – though his friends insist it was more of an embarrassed wave. Tragically, a year later, during the Belgian Grand Prix at Spa on 25 June 1939, Seaman was fatally injured driving in heavy rain. His last words to his wife were: 'I am afraid you must go to the cinema alone after all.' At the racing driver's funeral in London – just two months before the outbreak of war – Hitler paid his respects with an ostentatious floral tribute.

Was he killed by a secret Soviet underwater weapon? Or did he simply defect to the Russians? Maybe he was captured and brainwashed? Or more sinister still, was he murdered by MI6? Someone somewhere must surely know. The chances are that the rest of us never will. The strangest of Cold War dramas had washed up just outside Chichester, and to this day, the mystery of **Buster Crabb** remains intact.

In April 1956, the Russian cruiser *Ordzhonikidze* was in Portsmouth Harbour carrying the Soviet leaders Bulganin and Khrushchev to Britain for a formal visit. Crabb, a naval and MI6 frogman, entered the water three times to investigate the ship's design, the third time never to return. More than a year later, a headless body – later identified as Crabb – was found in Chichester Harbour. But far from solving the mystery, the discovery deepened it. More than half a century later, speculation is still our only recourse.

Goodwood emerged in the post-war years as an iconic centre for British motor racing, attracting big names and huge crowds in a golden era for the sport in this country. Sadly, it was at Goodwood, however, that motor racing lost one of its great heroes. The New Zealander **Bruce McLaren** was killed in a crash while testing a car on 2 June 1970. McLaren's name lives on in the successful Formula One team.

CHICHESTER CULTURE

Chichester Writers

Just as Chichester has long proved an inspiration to artists, so too has it inspired those who put pen to paper. Writers – like musicians and artists – are a central part of Chichester's heritage. Some were simply born here; others were drawn to the area by its beauties and fascinations.

The poet **William Collins** was born in Chichester in 1721, the son of a hatmaker and former mayor of the city. Educated at Winchester and Oxford, Collins moved to London in the 1740s but his literary efforts came to little and he returned to Chichester for the last years of his life, sinking into melancholy at the way his writings were received. Contemporary accounts talk of Collins's ravings, groanings and descent into madness. He died a broken man in Chichester on 12 June 1759, and was buried three days later in St Andrew's churchyard. Posthumously, his true literary merit has been acknowledged. For some, Collins is one of the finest English lyric poets of the eighteenth century. Works include *Odes on Several Descriptive and Allegorical Subjects* and the unfinished 'Ode on the Popular Superstitions of the Highlands of Scotland'. He is commemorated in Chichester Cathedral.

Born in Chichester on 9 November 1745, **William Hayley** was a poet, biographer and patron of the arts. It was Hayley who invited the poet and visionary William Blake to live in a cottage on his Felpham estate – a stay which ended with Blake's trial for sedition in Chichester. Hayley was also a supporter of the Chichester novelist Charlotte Smith. As a playwright, Hayley met with limited success. However, his works of scholarship fared rather better. He wrote notably on the subject of John Milton, and his *Life of Cowper* was published in 1803–1804 in five volumes. Hayley died in Felpham on 12 November 1820.

The poet and novelist **Charlotte Smith** (1749–1806) was born in London but sent to school in Chichester at the age of six. She returned to the city in later life. Smith's novels include *Emmeline* (1788) and *The Old Manor House* (1793).

Poet **Charles Crocker** (1797–1861) was born and died in Chichester. His works include *The Vale of Obscurity, The Lavant, and Other Poems* (1830) and *Kingley Vale and Other Poems* (1837). Other works include the guidebook *A Visit to Chichester Cathedral* (1849).

Brewer's Dictionary of Phrase and Fable has become a phrase in itself. It was one of a number of works written by **Ebenezer Cobham Brewer** (1810–1897), an educationist determined to make knowledge accessible. Brewer made his name with his *Guide to the Scientific Knowledge of Things Familiar* (*c*.1841), and his *Dictionary of Phrase and Fable* followed in 1870. Other works included his *Dictionary of Miracles* (1884). By the late 1860s, Brewer had made his home at Lavant. Later, he moved to Nottinghamshire to be with his daughter.

John Keats (1795–1821) started to write *The Eve of St Agnes* in Chichester in 1819 – a fact commemorated by a plaque above Eastgate Square.

Anna Sewell (1820–1878) began and ended her days in Norfolk, but in between, thanks to the demands of her father's employment, the family moved a good deal, spending a number of years in Sussex. They lived in Brighton from 1837 to 1845, Lancing from 1845 to 1849, Haywards Heath from 1849 to 1853 and in Graylingwell Farmhouse in Chichester from 1853 to 1858. *Black Beauty*, her only book, was published in 1877 and has entranced generations of horse-loving young readers ever since.

Matthew Phipps Shiel (1865–1947) was born in Montserrat in the West Indies and came to England to study. Thereafter he embarked on a series of colourful novels with big themes, rich in romanticism and full of adventure, of which perhaps the best known is *The Purple Cloud*. For a while he lived near Horsham. Shiel died on 17 February 1947 at St Richard's Hospital, Chichester.

Born on 29 March 1880, **Mabel Constanduros** was a popular figure in British radio comedy between the wars. A comedienne and writer, she lives on in memory principally for her creation of the country's first radio family, the Buggins family, in 1925. Between 1928 and 1948, Constanduros wrote and performed in more than 250 Buggins radio scripts. The series was particularly popular during World War Two. Constanduros died in the Royal West Sussex Hospital, Chichester, on 8 February 1957.

Writer and broadcaster **Gerald William Bullett** (1893–1958) had his first novel published in 1916 when he was serving with the Royal Flying Corps in France. Later works included *The History of Egg Pandervil* (1928) and *Nicky, Son of Egg* (1929). He remained prolific in the interwar years, and later works included *The Elderbrook Brothers* (1945), *The Alderman's Son* (1954), *The Daughters of Mrs Peacock* (1957) and *The Peacock Brides* (1958). He died in Chichester.

A child star on the stage before taking up the pen, **Esmé Wynne-Tyson** (1898–1972) was a prolific writer of non-fiction and journalism as well as fiction, often in collaboration. Her novels include *Security* (1927), *Quicksand* (1927), *Momus* (1928) and *Melody* (1929). She also wrote children's stories. Wynne-Tyson died at St Richard's Hospital, Chichester, on 17 January 1972.

Sir Harold Hobson (1904–1992) served as the drama critic for *The Sunday Times* from 1947 to 1976. In his early years in the post he championed poetic playwrights, including T. S. Eliot and Christopher Fry. Hobson also espoused the cause of French post-war theatre, notably in two books, *The French Theatre of Today* (1953) and *French Theatre since 1830* (1978). His autobiography *Indirect Journey* was published in 1978. Hobson spent his final days in Westhampnett Nursing Home near Chichester and died there on 12 March 1992.

For many years East Dean was home to the poet and playwright **Christopher Fry** (1907–2005). His most celebrated play *The Lady's Not for Burning* (1948) was revived in Chichester's Minerva Theatre in 2002. Fry attended the first night and was applauded by the cast at the end of the performance. Other works include *The Boy with a Cart* (1938), *A Phoenix Too Frequent* (1946), *A Sleep of Prisoners* (1951) and *The Dark Is Light Enough* (1954).

Robert Gittings (1911–1992) is perhaps best known for his literary biographies *John Keats* (1969), *The Young Thomas Hardy* (1975) and *The Older Hardy* (1978). Gittings also wrote a number of collections of poetry. Born in Southsea on 1 February 1911, he was a lifelong friend of his fellow East Dean resident Christopher Fry. Still fondly remembered for his efforts in recruiting cricket teams from Chichester Festival Theatre's actors, Gittings died in Chichester on 18 February 1992.

There was a time when every schoolchild read it. *The Silver Sword* is a classic children's story of wartime displacement. It was written by **Ian Serraillier** (1912–1994), author, schoolmaster and editor. Published in 1956, the book is the powerful tale of a family trying to reunite in the aftermath of World War Two, a time when the whole of Europe was a mass of people on the move. For many years, Serraillier lived at Singleton, just north of Chichester.

He died in a retirement home at Runcton, south-east of the city, on 28 November 1994.

The author who fired most schoolboys' enthusiasm for all things Roman was **Rosemary Sutcliff** (1920–1992) with her gripping *Eagle of the Ninth* series. A prolific writer, she gained legions of fans for her historical fiction and her children's literature. Sutcliff lived for many years at Walberton, between Chichester and Arundel, and died on 23 July 1992 at St Richard's Hospital, Chichester.

The poet and playwright **Ted Walker** (1934–2004) lived in Hunston and taught at Chichester High School in the 1960s. Born in Lancing, he was educated at Steyning and Cambridge. Notable works included his poetry collection *Fox on a Barn Door* (1965) and his account of his wife Lorna's death from cancer, *The Last of England* (1993). Walker was also a frequent contributor to the *Chichester Observer*.

Born in Whitton, Middlesex, in 1936, crime writer **Peter Lovesey** has made his home in Chichester. Lovesey's principal creation is the Bath-based detective Peter Diamond. He also wrote the Sergeant Cribb series of Victorian detective novels which were filmed as *Cribb* by Granada Television and ran from 1979 to 1981, starring Alan Dobie. Lovesey was the chairman of the Crime Writers' Association from 1991 to 1992 and received the CWA Cartier Diamond Dagger Lifetime Achievement Award in 2000.

Kate Mosse (born 1961) is a novelist, non-fiction writer and award-winning playwright. Chichester born and bred, she and her family divide their time between their homes in Chichester and Carcassonne, in the south-west of France, where her multi-million international No.1 best-selling novels are set. Mosse is the author of *Labyrinth*, *Sepulchre*, *The Winter Ghosts* and *Citadel*, the last of which was published in October 2012. Topping the charts for more than six months in 2006, *Labyrinth* won Best Read of 2006, has been translated into 38 languages, published in 40 countries and has been filmed for television by Ridley Scott starring John Hurt. In 2012, Mosse published *Chichester Festival Theatre at Fifty* – to commemorate the founding of CFT in 1961 – and is now working on a play for 2014. The co-founder and honorary director of the Women's Prize for Fiction (formerly the Orange Prize for Fiction), Mosse served as administrative director at Chichester Festival Theatre from 1998–2001 and is on the Board of the National Theatre in London.

Chichester Museums

With a rich history to celebrate, an important Chichester challenge has always been how best to display its heritage – a challenge definitively met in the summer of 2012.

Chichester set up its first museum in 1831, on the back of the Industrial Revolution, a time which brought with it a thirst for knowledge. With public donations of both exhibits and money, Dr John Forbes set up the museum as a natural history collection in the new **Royal West Sussex Hospital** which had opened just a few years before. Subsequent locations in the city included 7 North Pallant and 45

South Street. The museum flourished for a while, but visitor numbers dwindled, and the later years of the nineteenth century were a period of decline. The army commandeered the museum building in 1914, the year which saw the outbreak of World War One.

Chichester's next museum was the **Guildhall** in Priory Park, a building which had long played its part in the city's government and in its dispensing of justice. Built in the 1270s by the Franciscans, it was here that the writer William Blake was tried for sedition in 1804. A different role for the Guildhall started to emerge in 1936 when the building hosted a two-week exhibition. The following decade, the Guildhall was established as home to Chichester's museum.

However, the museum service found a more permanent home in the early 1960s with the intervention of Chichester architect Stanley Roth. An exhibition on 'Changing Chichester' was held in the Assembly Rooms in 1961. It proved a talking point. Roth bought the disused Sadler's corn store in **Little London** and came to an arrangement whereby the council leased it from him for a museum. The new Chichester Museum opened in 1963 and remained there for nearly fifty years. Under local government reorganisation, it became the District Museum in 1974.

The most recent chapter in Chichester's museum history began with the decision to relocate the District Museum to a new building on the site of the city's former Roman baths in Chichester's north-west quadrant, opposite Chichester Library. It was a move which gave the new museum a fascinating new showpiece, revealing properly to the public the baths which were first discovered in the 1970s by Chichester archaeologist Alec Down and his team of volunteers. The new museum, called **The Novium**, was opened in Tower Street in July 2012, embodying the very latest in museum thinking. The building was designed by multi-award-winning architect Keith Williams whose other projects include the Wexford Opera House in Ireland and the Unicorn Theatre in London. The museum stands on piles rather than foundations so as to protect the archaeology beneath it. Outside, the pale reconstructed stone was chosen to blend with the existing Chichester townscape; inside, the impression is strikingly modern, the result of a design process determined to maximise space and also the views the new building offers, particularly of Chichester Cathedral a couple of hundred yards to the south.

Chichester Men and Women of Vision

Every city is home to people who look beyond it. Chichester has played its part in the business, media and educational life of the country.

It takes a man of vision to create a dynasty – and to change the way a nation eats. Just such a man was Chichester's **Charles Shippam**. Shippam set up a grocery shop in Chichester's Westgate in 1786, and for the next two centuries, the Shippam family remained at the heart of the Chichester business community. Charles's son Charles Shippam II continued the family trade, as did Charles Shippam

III, opening a butcher's shop in East Street. In 1892 a factory was built behind the shop, producing the canned goods and potted meats with which the Shippam name became synonymous. Their potted meats and pastes were shown in London in 1896, a feather in the Shippam cap; and in the Boer War (1899–1902), Shippam's canned sausages were a staple for the troops.

In the business world, the name Shippam also stood for innovation. The company pioneered the use of a glass jar with a sealed metal lid for a longer shelf life and was among the first businesses to advertise on commercial television. However, Shippam's became part of the Grand Metropolitan group in 1995, and direct Shippam family involvement ended three years later. In August 2002, the East Walls factory closed, with production moving to Terminus Road.

Influential in a very different way was **Peter Lund Simmonds** (1814–1897), a man who took the word newsagent to unprecedented levels. From a base in Chichester, Simmonds secured newspapers and journals and sent them around the world. Born in Denmark, Simmonds was adopted by a naval family in Portsea Island and grew up to become the epitome of forward-thinking Victorian endeavour. The 1830s saw a great explosion in the number of publications and magazines; Simmonds, by now a journalist, saw an opportunity. In the late 1830s he set himself up as a 'newspaper agent' in Chichester, where he stayed until 1841.

In London, he pursued his own successful publishing career, all part of a network of communications he created worldwide. *Simmonds' Colonial Magazine*, *The Technologist: a Monthly Record of Science Applied to Art and Manufacture* and *The Journal of Applied Science* were among his successes. Sadly, though, he was to fall victim to another of the Victorian era's great innovations. Simmonds was knocked down by a bus and died two weeks later.

For **Emily Davies** (1830–1921), the thought that women should be denied the chance to study at university was intolerable. She became one of the country's most prominent promoters of higher education for women. Davies spent some of her early childhood years in Chichester where her father ran a school – an irony not lost on Emily when she considered the lack of serious schooling to which she was herself condemned.

In her twenties Davies became involved with the rather unfortunately named SPEW, the Society for Promoting the Employment of Women. But it was education, rather than employment, where she made her mark, campaigning for London University to offer degrees to women. It was to be a long process, but Davies was never daunted. Her most important book was *The Higher Education of Women* (1866); arguably, however, her lasting memorial is Girton College, Cambridge. She was instrumental in its creation. Davies's guiding principle wasn't simply that women should be admitted to higher education. She argued that they should be allowed to follow exactly the same courses open to men – something we now take for granted.

Dame Anita Roddick (1942–2007) combined principle and entrepreneurial flair in a way which enabled her to create an empire. One of the country's most remarkable businesswomen, Roddick inaugurated an approach to business that was as ethical as it was successful. Roddick opened the first Body Shop in Brighton in 1976; within a few years, she was authorising franchises across Europe. She personally promoted her product but never wavered from her crusading moral principles.

Roddick argued: 'The business of business should not just be about money, it should be about responsibility. It should be about public good, not private greed.' Under her influence, Body Shops carried posters supporting Greenpeace's anti-whaling campaign and collected signatures for a petition to save the Brazilian rainforest. She was voted Veuve Clicquot businesswoman of the year in 1984. By 1990 she was the fourth-richest woman in Britain. Born in Littlehampton on 23 October 1942, Roddick died at St Richard's Hospital, Chichester, on 10 September 2007, following a brain haemorrhage.

Perceptions of Chichester

Chichester in 1897

Chichester, the human city, the city of God, the place where life and work and things were all in one and all in harmony. That, without words, was how it appeared to me that day... It was a town, a city, a thing planned and ordered... I only know that Chichester was what Brighton was not, an end, a thing, a place, the product of reason and love. For here too love was visible. Here was no dead product of mathematical calculations, no merely sanitary and convenient arrangement. Here was something as human as home and as lovely as heaven. That was how it seemed to me, and I went back to Brighton on my bicycle in the evening glow of excitement.

Eric Gill (on the day in 1897 when he first saw Chichester), *Autobiography*, 1940

Chichester in 1915

It is an ideal place for anyone seeking a healthy, quiet old city wherein to reside, or to spend a quiet holiday being sheltered from the north by the Downs, while sea breezes are wafted from the south.

Not only does Chichester cater for the shopping needs of a large agricultural population, but it also is consistently patronised by an influential clientele whose exacting tastes have led the traders, in the majority of instances, carrying

*a stock of goods which not only in quality,
but in fashion and up-to-dateness, vie with
anything to be obtained in the Metropolis. The
traders as a class have earned a well-deserved
reputation for courtesy and efficiency of
service, and their wares bear an equally sound
reputation for honest value and reliability.*
CHICHESTER CITY GUIDE, 1915

Chichester in 1929

*...a dear, decorous Victorian lady of a
town. I do not mean this as an expression
of sarcasm but of admiration.*
R. THURSTON HOPKINS,
KIPLING'S SUSSEX REVISITED, 1929

Chichester Actors

Chichester's natural attractions – and for the past fifty years the presence of Chichester Festival Theatre (CFT) – have acted as a magnet to the acting community. Actors associated with the city present a veritable *Who's Who* of the profession.

Born in London on 14 July 1889, actress **Ruby Miller** died in Cawley Road, Chichester, on 2 April 1976. Miller appeared in a number of early films including *Little Women* (1917), *Edge o' Beyond* (1919), and *The Mystery of Mr Bernard Brown* (1921). In 1926 she appeared on the stage alongside a very young Laurence Olivier in *The Ghost Train* by Arnold

Ridley, later Private Godfrey in *Dad's Army* on TV. Miller's other films included *Power of Attorney* (1942) and *The Hundred Pound Window* (1944).

Born in Barnt Green, Worcestershire in 1922, **Margaret Leighton** died in Chichester on 13 January 1976. Leighton made her reputation on the stage, making her London debut in *Peer Gynt* (1944). She became a regular both in the West End and on Broadway. Her films included *The Astonished Heart* (1950), *The Winslow Boy* (1948), *The Sound and the Fury* (1959) and *The Go-Between* (1970). For many she remains the definitive Miss Havisham in Charles Dickens's *Great Expectations*, a part she played on television in 1974. She died at the age of fifty-three following a long battle with multiple sclerosis.

Born on 23 July 1912, **Michael Wilding** – Margaret Leighton's husband – survived her by three years. He died near Chichester on 8 July

1979, at the age of sixty-six. Notable film credits include *In Which We Serve* (1942). He also featured in *Piccadilly Incident* (1946), *The Courtneys of Curzon Street* (1947), *Spring in Park Lane* (1948), and *Maytime in Mayfair* (1949). After his marriage to Margaret Leighton in 1964, Wilding largely concentrated on furthering his wife's career.

Actress **Peggy Mount** (1915–2001) lost her sight while on stage in Chekhov's *Uncle Vanya* at Chichester in 1998 and had to give up acting. 'The audience had no idea. But... I lost my nerve... my greatest regret. It was always my wish to die working,' she told *The Independent*. She died three years later at the theatrical retirement home, Denville Hall, Northwood, London.

Jack Tripp (1922–2005), one of our greatest pantomime performers, made his last appearance at Chichester Festival Theatre. He appeared as Lord

Brockhurst in Sandy Wilson's 1930s pastiche *Divorce Me, Darling!* (1997).

Born on 11 September 1923, **Alan Badel** was regarded as one of the most captivating actors of his generation. Films included *This Sporting Life* (1963), *The Day of the Jackal* (1973) and *The Riddle of the Sands* (1979). Television roles included *Vanity Fair* (1956), Mr Darcy in *Pride and Prejudice* (1957), *Don Juan in Hell* (1962), *The Prisoner* (1963), *The Lover* (1963) and *The Count of Monte Cristo* (1964). He died at his home in St Martin's Square, Chichester, on 19 March 1982.

Patricia Routledge – star of *Keeping Up Appearances* and *Hetty Wainthropp Investigates* first came to Chichester to perform opposite her great hero Alastair Sim at the Festival Theatre in 1969. She recalls:

I came down here to play opposite one of my great idols, the wonderful Alastair Sim. It was a glorious summer. It was such a lovely way to spend the summer. I was in The Magistrate *which was Alastair at his peak. I was also in* The Country Wife *with Maggie Smith and I was in what we called* The Caucasian Church Social – *Brecht's* Caucasian Chalk Circle. *Somebody lent me a bike. I would cycle everywhere around the country lanes. There was not much traffic then, and whenever I thought of Chichester after that, I thought of Chichester in sunshine.*

INTERVIEW WITH THE AUTHOR, *CHICHESTER OBSERVER*, 27 MARCH 2007

Inevitably Chichester became her home, where she remains a passionate supporter of the arts. Subsequent roles at the CFT have included Lady Bracknell in *The Importance of Being Earnest* in the main house (1999), plus a memorable Beatrix Potter in *Beatrix* in the Minerva (1996). Routledge was born on 17 February 1929.

A firm favourite with the British public, **Diana Dors** (1931–1984) was in many ways a tragic figure, and it was at Chichester Festival Theatre in 1974 that Dors turned to tragedy on the stage. Her Jocasta in Sophocles's *Oedipus* was a rare stab at the classics and was moderately well received.

Edward Hardwicke made Chichester his home towards the end of his life. Arguably our greatest ever Watson (to Jeremy Brett's Holmes), Hardwicke was the son of screen idol Sir Cedric Hardwicke. Edward appeared at Chichester Festival Theatre in Sir Laurence Olivier's company in its very earliest days. Subsequent CFT appearances included Terence Rattigan's *The Winslow Boy*, in which he played the part of Mr Winslow, the father of a young naval cadet wrongly accused of stealing a five-shilling postal order. Hardwicke's father had played the role in the 1948 film version, and so it 'completed the circle' for Edward to play it in Chichester in 2001, especially as it was in Chichester in 1964 that Olivier broke the news to Edward of his father's death. Edward's own films included *Shadowlands* (1993), *Richard III* (1995) and *Elizabeth* (1998). Other memorable credits included the landmark World War Two television series *Colditz* (1972–1974). Born on 7 August 1932, he died in Chichester on 16 May 2011.

Coronation Street actor **Peter Baldwin** – best known as the soap's Derek Wilton – was born in Chichester on 29 July 1933.

Christopher Timothy, born 14 October 1940, is another actor who has made his home in the Chichester area after being drawn to the city by its theatre. His very time first on the Festival Theatre stage was in the CFT's third season in the landmark production of *The Royal Hunt of the Sun*, directed by John Dexter (1964). He remembers a beautiful summer in the days when the only buildings on site were the theatre and the offices, long before the Minerva was built. Similarly happy are Timothy's recollections of *Underneath the Arches*, for which he returned to the theatre in 1981. It was then that he met his Cicestrian wife Annie. They lived in Brighton for two or three years and have lived in the Chichester area ever since. Timothy's most celebrated TV role was James Herriot in *All Creatures Great and Small* (1978–1980 and 1988–1990).

The Chichester area has long been home to **Sarah Badel**, daughter of the late Alan Badel. In a long association with Chichester Festival Theatre, Badel's roles have included *An Italian Straw Hat* (1967) and *Cabaret (2002).* Film roles have included *The Shooting Party* (1985) and *Mrs Dalloway* (1997).

Anthony Andrews, an actor with strong Chichester ties, returned to the city in 2012 to appear as Prime Minister Anthony Eden in Hugh Whitemore's political thriller *A Marvellous Year For Plums*. Bizarrely, it was promotion from within the ranks of the *Chichester Observer* which had launched Andrews into his acting career forty-five years earlier in 1967. Seeing his image in the newspaper, Andrews had a moment of sudden revelation. He recalls:

> *The day I walked down to the theatre and asked for a job was because I was sitting in the advertising department at the* Chichester Observer *selling advertising space. I was given the task of creating a 'wine and dine' page that I had to sell to restaurants. I had to drive around the area selling the space, and because I was given this page, they printed my picture in the paper – 'Here is your new advertising manager!' Other people were listed alongside this mugshot of me, and I just looked at it and thought 'This is not what I want to do!' I thought 'Why am I here!' I remember that lunchtime asking at the stage door of the theatre whether there were any jobs going.*
> INTERVIEW WITH THE AUTHOR, *CHICHESTER OBSERVER*, 2 MAY 2012

Michael Elphick was a Chichester man through and through. A student at the city's Lancastrian School, he became involved with the Chichester Amateur Dramatic Society. He recalled:

> *I was in a play called* The Lady's Not For Burning *that we performed at the Assembly Rooms in North Street. I was about fifteen years old at the time. That was the year they were building this new theatre in Chichester. I often used to go up there to watch them building it. I had a paper round and part of my round was Franklin Place, so from there I could see the theatre going up. And then I left school, having done not very well, and got a job on the site just navvying. I was then taken on as an apprentice electrician working on the lights, which is when I met Laurence Olivier.*
>
> INTERVIEW WITH THE AUTHOR, *CHICHESTER OBSERVER*, 25 FEBRUARY 1999

Olivier encouraged him, and Elphick's career was underway. Most notably, Elphick played the title role in the private investigator series *Boon*. He was also Harry Slater in the BBC's *EastEnders*. Born on 19 September 1946, he died on 7 September 2002, aged 55.

Foyle's War star **Honeysuckle Weeks** – Eliza Doolittle in the 2010 production of *Pygmalion* at Chichester Festival Theatre – regards the Chichester area as home turf. Born in 1979, she grew up near Petworth and started her acting career with Chichester Festival Youth Theatre in 1988. She recalls:

> *I got everything from the Youth Theatre. It was a great learning experience. You learn how to conduct yourself backstage and how to go out there into an auditorium full of faces. You really are doing it for real in front of massive audiences. You learn how to be on stage, how to be free, how to be uninhibited, how to use your energy and your enthusiasm.*
>
> INTERVIEW WITH THE AUTHOR, *CHICHESTER OBSERVER*, 24 JUNE 2010

Chichester Today:
Facts and Figures

Longevity, low incidence of crime and comparative prosperity were all confirmed in a major study entitled *Chichester: A Community Profile*, which was published in 2002. The study took Chichester to mean effectively the Chichester District, including the towns of Midhurst and Petworth to the north of the city, and the coastal villages of Selsey and East and West Wittering to the south – a total of 106,445 people across 812 square kilometres.

The study found that:

- The population density is extremely low compared to the rest of the county and reflects the rural geography. There are more males than females up to the age of about nineteen. Between the ages of nineteen and fifty, the pattern varies. After the age of fifty, females outnumber males, especially in the 'over eighty-five' bracket where females outnumber the males 2:1.

- Tourism, retail trades and financial and administrative services provide plenty of employment. 'In October 2002, 86.3 per cent of people of working age were in employment, compared to a county-wide average of 83.7 per cent,' the study noted. However, Chichester has the second-lowest average level of earnings in West Sussex, perhaps because of low pay in hotels and restaurants.

- Chichester is a healthy place to live. The high death rates simply reflect the age of the population. 'Death rates of people under 75, including all the major causes of death, are consistently below the national norms,' the study recorded. Chichester as a whole has a life expectancy for both men and women slightly above the average for the county and well above the national average.

(SOURCE: *CHICHESTER: A COMMUNITY PROFILE* PREPARED AND PUBLISHED BY THE UNIVERSITY OF BRIGHTON, CARE EQUATION LIMITED AND THE SUSSEX RURAL COMMUNITY COUNCIL, OCTOBER 2002)

Figures from the 2001 Census (Office of National Statistics) state that the city covers 1,066.6 hectares, with a total population of 23,700 and an average 2.2 people per household.

The Census confirmed:

8 primary schools with 1,786 pupils

3 secondary schools with 4,290 pupils

2 special educational needs schools with 309 pupils

Chichester can boast a triple importance, as home to Chichester City Council, Chichester District Council and West Sussex County Council. For nearly a thousand years, it has also been home to Chichester Cathedral, the mother church of the Diocese of

Chichester, which covers East and West Sussex. Chichester also retains a judicial importance as home to Chichester Magistrates Court and Chichester Crown Court.

Chichester City Council can trace its first charter back to 1135. The City Council is the parish council for the city of Chichester. It is based at The Council House, North Street, Chichester (www.chichestercity.gov.uk).

Chichester District Council was set up in 1974 to cover an area that stretches from Petworth to the sea and from Westbourne in the west to Bury in the east. It provides services for nearly 110,000 people, with responsibilities that include waste collection, planning and building control, and leisure, sport and tourism. It is based at East Pallant House, East Pallant, Chichester (www.chichester.gov.uk).

West Sussex County Council dates back to 1888 and is responsible for services to 750,000 people across the county. Its services include libraries, highways, social services, education and fire. It is based at County Hall, West Street, Chichester (www.westsussex.gov.uk).

The Age of the Cinema

Cinemas past and present are part of the Chichester cityscape. The city's earliest cinemas have now gone, their place taken by a popular independent cinema housed in a former school and by a flourishing new multiplex.

The **Olympia Electric Theatre**, Chichester's first full-time picture house, was once a Mecca for a city seeking the newfangled delights of cinema. With a roller-skating rink next door, it opened in 1910 and, in its heyday, it was ornately decorated, offering all the comforts as Chichester caught up with a new art form which was to dominate so much of the twentieth century. Sadly, the story of the city's Olympia Electric Theatre wasn't to be a happy one. It suffered severe fire damage and closed in 1926. The building was later used as the Southdown bus garage. It is currently used for storage purposes. Forlorn on the Northgate roundabout, it sits neglected on the traffic island which grew up around it.

Chichester had, however, gained a new cinema with the opening of the **Odeon** in South Street in around 1920. The building is now home to the frozen-food store Iceland, but it doesn't take too much of a leap of the imagination to sense the cinema which once stood there – especially if you talk to the Cicestrians who fondly remember the hours they spent queuing outside in eager anticipation. It began life as the Picturedrome, but this was then demolished to make way for The Plaza which then became the Odeon. Its misfortune, however, was that it operated at a time when Chichester boasted three cinemas. Something had to give, and the Odeon closed down in February 1960.

Now it is Next; before that it was McDonald's; but for many Cicestrians the former Corn Exchange building in East Street will always be the **Granada** cinema. The building was home to entertainers, including the performers known as the Chichester Minstrels, in the late nineteenth century, and by 1910 films were screened there on a regular basis. It became a full-time cinema in 1922 and won a place in many Chichester hearts as the very best place to catch the latest releases. Premieres may have been in London, but Chichester's Granada was never far behind. Its cleverness was that it caught its audiences young, offering the full Saturday morning cinema experience to thousands of Chichester children. Eventually it fell victim to declining audiences and showed its last film in 1980.

Nothing remains now of Chichester's **Gaumont** cinema on Eastgate Square except the memory. It opened with a flourish on 20 September 1937 with a gala screening of *King Solomon's Mines* starring screen idol Sir Cedric Hardwicke, but audiences fell away over the years, and the cinema shut down in October 1960. The cinema had to compete with the

Granada just a few yards away in East Street and also with the Odeon, a couple of minutes' walk away in South Street. The Gaumont and the Odeon closed within months of each other. By 1967, the Gaumont had been gutted and the building reopened as a swimming pool. It proved popular throughout the 1970s, but was superseded by the new Westgate Leisure Centre to the south-west of the city centre, which opened in 1987. An Indian restaurant then

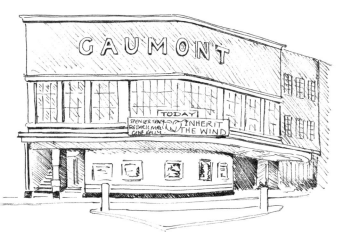

occupied the upper floor for a number of years, while the space downstairs served a number of uses including as a drop-in centre for the homeless. Eventually the site was cleared as part of the Eastgate Square redevelopment which created both housing and a range of new retail outlets. Where cinemagoers once flocked, there now stands Carluccio's Italian restaurant.

In the early years of the new millennium, Chichester gained its first-ever multiplex on the new Chichester Gate Leisure Park, just south of the city centre, a development on a site once partially occupied by the city's High School for Girls. The whole notion was years in the planning, but with the high number of empty restaurants at Chichester Gate these days, many would say that the complex has not yet managed to establish itself in the way originally intended. But a constant and popular presence from the start has been **Cineworld Chichester**. Its arrival gave the city its first taste of the big US-style multi-screen experience and meant an end to travelling for Cicestrians in search of the latest blockbusters.

Arguably, Chichester's cinematic gem is the **Chichester Cinema at New Park**, a place its devotees simply love to go. Housed in a former school just outside the city walls on the eastern side of Chichester, the independent cinema survives year after year on the back of intelligent programming and the enthusiasm of its audiences. They can see the big films there, but they can also enjoy the art-house movies the multiplexes won't touch. Just as importantly, they can enjoy an individualised cinema-going experience that multi-screen venues simply cannot offer. The main auditorium has 120 seats; the smaller studio space offers 40. On the back of this, the Chichester Cinema at New Park has become home to the Chichester International Film Festival, which in 2012 celebrated its twenty-first anniversary, under founding artistic director Roger Gibson. The festival began as a humble six-day affair during the city's annual July Festivities before moving to its own slot in August the following year. Since then, it has confirmed itself as a major event on the national calendar, offering a host of previews and premieres backed up by a strong programme of retrospectives, talks and other events. When Chichester gained its multiplex, many feared for the future of the Chichester Cinema at New Park. There was no need. Offering something different was always going to be New Park's great strength.

The Horrors of War: 1939–1945

Chichester escaped the devastation wreaked on Britain's big cities by German bombers during World War Two, but it certainly didn't escape the war. The south coast was the home front's front line; and in the early days of the war the invasion threat was real, until the Battle of Britain effectively secured our shores in the summer of 1940. Many Cicestrians recall seeing the dogfights overhead as air supremacy was decided in the Allies' favour during that fateful summer. The fact is that for Chichester the war was never far away.

When London came to Chichester…

World War Two arrived promptly in Chichester in the shape of scores of London evacuees. War was declared in September 1939, and that very same month little Londoners were already swapping the big city for a very different life in Chichester.

Among the influx were pupils of the Henry Thornton School in Clapham who boarded with Chichester families by night, and by day continued their education at Chichester High School for Boys (from October 1939 to July 1943). Nine of them returned to Chichester in 2009 to mark the seventieth anniversary of their evacuation to the south coast. Terry Sharp, then aged eighty-two, from London, was the youngest of the group to visit. He recalled:

> *It was great fun visiting the old parts of the school that we recognised. It evoked memories of our schooldays, and we got chatting about what lessons were taught and the masters who led the school.*
> CHICHESTER OBSERVER, 19 OCTOBER 2009

One particular memory was that if the air-raid siren went off before 5 p.m., it meant no homework that day.

The HTS teaching staff at CHSB included: W. D. Evans – headmaster; R. S. Bramble – physical education; A. H. Collins – English; W. J. Cooper – Latin; L. B. Cundall – geography; and G. W. Dix – art.

It wasn't long, however, before some of the London children started drifting back to the capital. In London, the Henry Thornton School had A, B and C forms in each year; in Chichester, they had just one form per year as numbers dwindled. But those who did remain at least had the consolation of a visit from Queen Elizabeth (who was to become the Queen Mother in 1952), on 11 December 1939.

The High School for Boys wasn't the only Chichester area school involved. A number of village schools, nearby Birdham included, became reception areas for London children. In many schools, where space and staffing were issues, local children were taught in the morning and the evacuees in the afternoon. In Chichester, overcrowding at the High School for Girls meant that part of the Bishop's Palace was used. Briefly, the children had the run of the Bishop's Palace Garden – a freedom rapidly curtailed once it became clear that the garden was hardly set up for dozens of youngsters. Instead, nature walks – taking in Brandy Hole Copse or across the Westgate fields – became a rather more marshalled way of coping with overcrowded classrooms.

In 1941, the future Prime Minister **Anthony Eden** took the lease on a seventeenth-century house at Binderton, near Chichester. By then, however, Eden and his wife Beatrice were leading largely separate lives – a separation increased by the fact that Eden's wartime duties meant he lived much of the time in a flat at the Foreign Office. Their country home didn't bring them together, and the couple divorced in 1950.

Family tragedy as bombs drop

Death fell from the skies on a grim day in 1943 when four bombs dropped on Chichester.

Margaret Mitchell left her home in Chapel Street, Chichester, for her weekly wartime treat – a Wednesday afternoon trip to the pictures. When she got home, her house was a pile of rubble. Five members of her family – including her eighteen-month-old daughter – were dead. Baby Brenda's shoes and part of her pram were found in Priory Park 500 yards away.

Her husband Alfred was just outside Algiers at the time, serving with the First Army. It was six weeks before he learnt what had happened. At a stroke, Mr Mitchell had lost three generations of his family. His mother Margaret was dead; so too were his daughter and his grandfather George. Also killed were his aunt Hilda Tester and her five-year-old daughter Vera. Mr Mitchell recalled:

The officer just called me into the office and told me. It was a shock, but you don't really react in those circumstances. They did try to help me as much as they could. They let me lie in a bit and everybody was very good. But I certainly couldn't go home. I tried, but there was a war on. I couldn't get home at all. There was no hope of that. The reason I couldn't was because my wife was not injured. She was saved because she had gone to the pictures. After eighteen months or whatever, you start to get over it. There was a war on, and you have to think of other things. Unless you have been in a war, you won't understand. I can't explain what it's like, but in a way it helped.

Interview with the author, *Chichester Observer*, 26 August 1999

Chichester was bombed three times during World War Two: Basin Road in 1941, Chapel Street and St Martin's Street in 1943 and Armadale Road and Green Lane in 1944. But Cicestrians will still tell you of the red sky all too frequently visible in the distance over Portsmouth, a sign that once again the city – a major port – was suffering at the hands of the Luftwaffe.

The day the Liberator crashed on Chichester

The astonishing thing is that only three people died on a grim day which could have been so much worse. It was 11 May 1944 and a stricken American **Liberator** bomber was heading back to Britain – a fatal journey which saw it crash and explode over Chichester, sending debris across a wide radius and shooting flames several hundred feet high.

The bomber came down on the allotments in Velyn Avenue, behind Kenneth Long and Company's timber yard, near the site of the old Roman amphitheatre, just south of The Hornet. Another 50 yards, and the chances are that none of the fifty to sixty workers in City Electric Laundry would have survived (only two laundry workers and a man working on his nearby allotment were killed) – a remarkable day which counts as both tragedy and near miss in the World War Two history of Chichester.

The plane had set off for a bombing raid over France where it was badly shot up. It came back in over Selsey Bill, but with fire raging on board, the pilot, Lt Joe Duncan, sensed disaster. He ordered the rest of the crew to bail out, turned the plane round to head out back to sea and then bailed out himself, only to see the engine fail on one side. Pilotless, the plane circled back toward Chichester where it crashed near the amphitheatre site. The explosion was enormous. Lt Duncan later wrote to his father:

I told my crew to prepare to bail out and I picked out a field in case a forced landing became necessary, but intending to go on home if the fire went out. It didn't. A few seconds later my engineer reported the fire had spread to the bomb bay and to the back of the plane, also No. 4 engine went out about that time, so I told the crew to bail out. Two of my boys had been fighting the fire with a hand extinguisher; they very neatly laid the extinguisher back in the radio compartment and left. The others were already leaving.

A few seconds and they were all gone, I called to make sure and at the same time I had been turning to get the 'ole wagon back to the Channel, only a little more and her nose was headed to sea so I decided it was time for me to go and did. A few seconds later the old girl exploded with a hell of a bang. Her tanks had exploded. It made me sick to see it 'cause as soon as I left her she turned right back and exploded right over a little town. Though the biggest pieces left after exploding were the engines, she did a lot of damage.

Chichester empties as D-Day dawns

Everyone knew something was brewing; the only question was when. And then, all of a sudden, the fields around Chichester were empty again.

The central south coast was the launch pad for the great amphibious landings recorded in history as D-Day, 6 June 1944, the moment the tide of war in Europe started to turn.

Chichester played its part. The build-up of servicemen in woods and fields around the area was immense and couldn't possibly go unnoticed. Many Cicestrians of a certain age recall that there were soldiers everywhere waiting for the off; and then the big day dawned. Tanks rumbled through the city; the skies darkened as countless planes and gliders passed overhead.

But the area was more than just a holding ground. There were practice landings on the beaches of the Witterings in May 1944 – all part of the Chichester district's wider role.

General Eisenhower stayed at The Ship Hotel in Chichester in 1944. It was at nearby Southwick House that the future President of the United States of America (1953–1961) masterminded the planning and preparation for D-Day.

If you had been able to perch on top of the spire of Chichester Cathedral in the spring of 1944, you would have seen no fewer than nine airfields. Tangmere, Westhampnett, Merston, Ford and Thorney Island were the established airfields. Funtington, Apuldram, Selsey and Bognor were temporary airfields known as Advanced Landing Grounds, created when it became obvious that greater back-up would be needed for the Normandy landing forces.

On the day, the nerve centre which controlled D-Day's squadrons of fighter planes was one of the lecture rooms in the city's Bishop Otter College, now the Bishop Otter campus of the University of Chichester.

Victory at last!

Along with the rest of the nation, Chichester celebrated the end of the war in Europe on 8 May 1945, but it did so with typical conscientiousness. Chichester wasn't going to be taken by surprise on VE Day, the day which marked the collapse of the Nazi war machine.

The mayor, Alderman Stride, had long since persuaded the city council to set up a committee to help arrange the celebrations. The committee conceded that it would have to allow free rein to spontaneity when victory finally came, but it insisted that planning was important too. A week before VE Day, Cicestrians were seen handing out flags; and then on the afternoon of Monday, 7 May, the city got the go-ahead it craved.

Streamers were put across the main streets; traders and businessmen started decorating their premises. The city became a blaze of colour. As the *Chichester Observer* in its 12 May edition the following Saturday wrote: 'There was a gaiety abroad among a good many who were impatient to start the merry-making.'

VE Day dawned brightly; and by 3 p.m. there was a great crowd around the City Cross to hear the relaying of Churchill's now historic VE Day speech with its imposing 'Advance, Britannia!' finale. 'The assembly round the cross became denser and denser, growing during the evening until it became positively prodigious,' the *Chichester Observer* noted.

Meanwhile, church services marked the nation's deliverance at 7 p.m.; Chichester City Band played at the cross until 9 p.m. as civilians and servicemen and women mingled. 'One party of young khaki-clad men formed a ring at one spot and started a dance on their own. Laughter and good humour held the field everywhere,' the *Chichester Observer* recorded.

The paper summed it all up when it hit the streets the following Saturday:

> *We have lived through a week of so many*
> *exciting and important events that we have*
> *hardly had time yet to come to earth and*
> *realise fully how much it all means.*

*After nearly six years of restricted existence,
full of the danger, strain and anxiety of
the greatest war ever, our country and her
allies have overthrown the mighty power of
aggressive Germany and forced her to that
unconditional surrender which Hitler once
boasted would never happen.*

*The threat to our freedom has vanished, and
the feelings of gratitude and relief which have
found expression in this week's rejoicings must
carry us a stage further to a solemn realisation
of the reality of the danger which has gone,
and to a fixed determination to take up our
freedom bravely and strive so to reshape it
that those who come after us will never be
confronted with such an ordeal again.*

When he covered the coronation of Queen Elizabeth II in 1953, radio and television broadcaster Richard Dimbleby (1913–1965) operated from his Dutch sailing barge *Vabel*, which he had brought round from Chichester and moored in the Thames. Dimbleby had been the first correspondent to enter the Belsen concentration camp in 1945, revealing its horrors to the world. He had also broadcast from Hitler's chair amid the rubble of the Führer's study in the Chancellery in Berlin.

Bishop Bell of Chichester: a Man of Peace

One of the twentieth century's great ecumenicists, **George Kennedy Allen Bell**, was born on Hayling Island in Hampshire on 4 February 1883. Ordained in 1907, he became chaplain to Archbishop Randall Davidson in 1914, was made Dean of Canterbury Cathedral in 1925 and appointed Bishop of Chichester in 1929.

For many, he was Chichester's greatest bishop, a man of immense compassion and spirituality, a man of unswerving courage and the highest moral principles. For others, he was a traitor. When in wartime he spoke out against the Allies' saturation bombing of German civilian targets, it wasn't just the letters page of the *Chichester Observer* that was filled with fury. The controversy was huge – and may ultimately have cost Bishop Bell the primacy. Bell's supporters believed

him uniquely equipped to serve as Archbishop of
Canterbury. Many have argued that it was the nation's
loss that he was not appointed to the office.

Christian unity was the key feature of his life's
work. A strong supporter of the World Council of
Churches, Bell forewarned of the evils of Nazism and
developed strong ties with the German Confessing
Church, opponents of Hitler's regime. During
the war he campaigned for British support for the
German resistance movement. Bell was a close
friend of Dietrich Bonhoeffer, the German dissident
pastor who was executed by the Nazis just weeks
before the capitulation of Germany in 1945.

Bell was implacable towards what he saw as the evil of obliteration bombing. Writing to *The Times* in 1941, he condemned the indiscriminate bombing of German cities as 'barbarian'. His argument was that the bombing of unarmed women and children robbed the Allies of the moral high ground they surely needed to fight from. On several occasions he spoke out in the House of Lords:

The policy is obliteration, openly acknowledged. This is not a justifiable act of war...

How can the War Cabinet fail to see that this progressive devastation of cities is threatening the roots of civilisation? Does the Government understand the full force of what area bombardment is doing and is destroying now? Are they alive not only to the vastness of the material damage, much of which is irreparable, but also to the harvest they are laying up for the future relationships of the peoples of Europe, as well as to its moral implications?

SPEECH, HOUSE OF LORDS, 9 FEBRUARY 1944.

After the war, Bell worked tirelessly to re-establish links between the English and German churches. He also travelled as both chairman and president of the World Council of Churches. Bell announced his retirement as Bishop of Chichester on 4 June 1957 and died in Canterbury on 3 October 1958. Continuing his work, Chichester Cathedral now runs George Bell House as a centre for vocation, education and reconciliation.

Mahatma Gandhi and Chichester are not words often seen in the same sentence. The connection in the autumn of 1931 was Bishop George Bell, who invited Gandhi to West Sussex. The *Chichester Observer* may have missed the significance of his visit, giving it considerably less space in the paper than the horse racing at Fontwell. It is said that Gandhi brought a goat with him and tethered it on the cathedral green though this story may be apocryphal. While in Chichester, Gandhi also visited C. P. Scott, the great editor of *The Guardian*. Scott's sister lived a few miles away at Bognor Regis, and Gandhi met them there for lunch.

T. S. Eliot (1888–1965) was commissioned by George Bell to write the church drama *Murder in the Cathedral*, which portrayed the assassination of Thomas Beckett. It was performed in Canterbury Cathedral in June 1935 as part of the Canterbury Festival. Bell had served as Dean of Canterbury from 1925 to 1929.

Bishop of Liverpool and former Sussex and England cricketer **David Sheppard** (1929–2005) was ordained by Bishop Bell of Chichester. One of Sheppard's many distinctions is that he is the only ordained minister to have played Test cricket.

But Was It Really a Slum?

Chichester is today rightly lauded for its Georgian splendours, but hindsight suggests it might just have let some of them slip through its fingers. In the early 1960s, a whole community was lost with the demolition of the **Somerstown** area, to the north of the city centre, under the guise of post-war slum clearance. The parts of Somerstown which survived are now regarded as gems containing much-sought-after properties which sell for high prices. The irony is that the houses that escaped the bulldozer are now listed and protected, a pattern found in cities across England where post-war redevelopment in many instances arguably ignored pre-war heritage.

Somerstown was an area of six streets outside the city walls, largely housing working-class and artisan families. The idea was that they would meet the needs of the affluent residents living inside the walls.

Dating back to the early 1800s, Somerstown was a busy, self-supporting neighbourhood, home to nine pubs and a host of shops and businesses, including grocers, bakeries, a snack bar and even an antique shop. Throughout its history, it was a low-income area, but families had lived there for generations, and the sense of community was strong, even as the gap progressively widened between post-war expectations and the quality of the accommodation on offer.

Many of the houses had no heating, no bathroom, an outside toilet and only two bedrooms – shortfalls which seemed increasingly glaring as the 1960s dawned. In places, money was certainly scarce, and a good number of the houses were in a poor state of repair. But whatever state the properties were in, for their occupants, their house was home.

In accordance with government recommendations, the city council announced a five-year programme of slum clearance and redevelopment in 1955: 426 houses were marked down for demolition, including many in Somerstown. Some residents were delighted to move on; others were adamant that they were staying. The council had to resort to compulsory purchase to force some people out. As the houses emptied, so the demolition started.

Two-thirds of Somerstown – the houses on the eastern side of St Paul's Road – were pulled down. Parchment, Washington and Cavendish Streets – the final third on the western side – survived and are now considered highly desirable addresses. Those who still lament the demolition insist that restoration and refurbishment were the answers, not a sledgehammer. As former resident Joyce McKenzie put it:

> *We lost a large area of very characterful Georgian properties, but importantly we lost a very large community of more than five hundred people, a very close-knit thriving community that was dispersed throughout the city. I can't really say what the reason was the council knocked it down. They said the demolished houses were slums, but they were built at exactly the same time as the ones in Parchment, Washington and Cavendish streets which were all in much the same condition. At one time, Parchment, Washington and Cavendish streets were all intended to be demolished as well, but then they changed their minds. Our house wasn't a slum at all. We owned our house. Most of the houses around were rented, but I can't find anybody who was pleased to move out.*
> INTERVIEW WITH THE AUTHOR, *CHICHESTER OBSERVER*, 2009

In the eyes of some, the demolition even contributed to the current housing shortfall:

Nobody denies that there is a shortage of small houses in this city today. In addition to the usual reasons for downsizing, the credit crunch makes them even more desirable. This shortage is partly due to the folly of the planners in the early 1960s when they permitted the bulldozing of around 250 modest homes in Somerstown.

THE CHICHESTER SOCIETY NEWSLETTER,
MARCH 2009

The Legacy of Walter Hussey

Chichester Cathedral has long had a reputation for its encouragement of the arts – a reputation furthered by the work of one of the cathedral's most celebrated deans, Walter Hussey (1909–1985). Hussey believed that:

Art of high standard can and should be offered to God and in the offering symbolise all that should be offered by mankind.

It was a belief he put into practice. While vicar of St Matthew's Church in Northampton, Hussey commissioned Henry Moore's *Madonna and Child* (1944) and Graham Sutherland's *Crucifixion* (1946). At Hussey's encouragement, Benjamin Britten, Michael Tippett, Lennox Berkeley and Malcolm Arnold also created works for his church.

Hussey was appointed Dean of Chichester Cathedral in 1955, where he remained until 1977. While in Chichester, he commissioned a tapestry for the altar reredos from John Piper (1966) and a stained-glass window from Marc Chagall (1978). Ceri Richards designed a set of copes (1960), and Graham Sutherland painted *Noli me tangere* for Chichester in 1961.

Cultural historian Kenneth Clark regarded Hussey as the Church of England's last great patron of the arts. Hussey saw art as an important weapon in the spiritual arsenal of 'Christian civilization', a crucial buffer against totalitarianism.

Walter Hussey left his personal collection to Chichester in 1977, with the condition that it be shown in Pallant House, the Grade 1 listed Queen Anne town house dating from 1712.

Pallant House Gallery opened in 1982, but for many years severe lack of space meant that it could show just a fraction of its permanent collection at

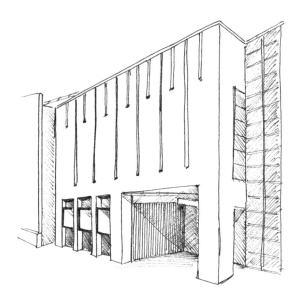

any one time; and so pressure grew for the modern extension which opened in 2006 alongside vastly improved facilities.

In the years since its relaunch, Pallant House Gallery has confirmed its place as home to one of the best collections of modern British art in the UK. Exhibitions of the permanent collection are complemented by regularly changing temporary exhibitions and a busy programme of workshops, talks, tours and live performances.

A crowning moment for the new-look gallery came in 2007 when it won the prestigious Gulbenkian Prize for museums and galleries, beating off three other contenders on the shortlist including London's Kew Palace. Francine Stock, chairman of the Gulbenkian Prize, commented:

> *A jewel of a gallery. The brilliance of Pallant House Gallery lies not only in its thoughtful and intelligent curation but in the warmth and welcome of the building. There's nothing elitist about the way this fine collection is displayed – intimate yet with space for reflection and tranquillity.*

Hussey's legacy seems assured for the future.

CHICHESTER CULTURE

Seeing Stars: Leslie Evershed-Martin

You would expect an ophthalmic optician to be a man of vision, but not many take it to the lengths Chichester's Leslie Evershed-Martin did in the middle years of the twentieth century. Evershed-Martin looked into the future, saw a theatre in Chichester and made it happen.

Evershed-Martin recalled that he was sitting at home on a blustery night in January 1959 when the idea came to him. He was half-reading, half-viewing as broadcaster Huw Wheldon appeared on the television screen to present his programme *Monitor*, in which he reviewed the latest achievements in the arts. In this particular episode, Wheldon focused on the Festival Theatre in Stratford, Ontario, Canada, home to the annual Stratford Shakespeare Festival, and interviewed the celebrated theatrical producer Sir Tyrone Guthrie. As he recalled in his memoir *The Impossible Theatre*, Evershed-Martin found himself 'enthralled' at the tale of community effort which lay behind the whole venture. He promptly started to plan something similar for Chichester:

> *I could see the immense dramatic possibilities of the thrust stage, where the audience were no longer peering into a room at its occupants but were, in effect, in there with them.*
>
> THE IMPOSSIBLE THEATRE,
> PHILLIMORE & CO, 1971

The concept of festival was crucial, a summer-only opening that left people wanting more. Evershed-Martin saw it as imperative that audiences must never be allowed to think 'I must go there sometime'; instead, the festival theatre season had to bring with it a huge sense of occasion which compelled audiences to book now if they wanted to come.

Evershed-Martin was a persuasive man. He gained allies, and the project gained momentum. On 1 July

1959 Evershed-Martin, a former mayor of Chichester, put the idea of a theatre to Chichester City Council sitting *in camera*. They agreed in principle a ninety-nine-year lease at a peppercorn rent for the Oaklands Park site Evershed-Martin had in mind, just to the north of the city centre. Designs were drawn up by distinguished architects Philip Powell and Hidalgo Moya, and fundraising began in earnest. Evershed-Martin's son David recalled:

> *The main memory I have is of father coming back almost each day. He would be ringing people and asking to come and see them and tell them about the theatre, and it became an extraordinary wave-like motion. He would be up one day when he came back and the next day he would be down. There was this strange good and bad wave pattern. We certainly had moments when we were worried.*
>
> INTERVIEW WITH THE AUTHOR,
> *CHICHESTER OBSERVER*, 2003

A turning point came when Evershed-Martin secured **Sir Laurence Olivier** as the theatre's founding artistic director. He cabled the great man: 'The Sussex Downs will shout with joy to welcome you.' Princess Alexandra laid the foundation stone on 12 May 1961, the new building started to take shape, and on 10 January 1962, Olivier announced his first season – a nine-week festival comprising *The Chances*, *The Broken Heart* and *Uncle Vanya*, with a cast to include Sir Lewis Casson, Fay Compton, Joan Greenwood, Keith Michell, John Neville, Sir Laurence Olivier himself, Joan Plowright, Sir Michael Redgrave, Athene Seyler and Dame Sybil Thorndike, with Olivier directing all three plays and appearing in the last two.

The building was finished on 3 May 1962, and on 4 June Olivier welcomed the actors to Chichester. Evershed-Martin was ecstatic: 'I told them we had aimed at the stars, but had never expected the whole firmament' (*The Impossible Theatre*). On 5 July 1962, the theatre opened with a first night which could have sold out three times over. Evershed-Martin's vision had been realised. John Gale, CFT executive producer 1983–1984 and CFT artistic director 1985–1989, recalls:

> *In forty years of working in the theatre, I can say that Leslie Evershed-Martin is the only amateur I ever came across who had a deep understanding of the theatre. Where he got it from, where it came from, God alone knows. He was an ophthalmic optician. But he had an innate knowledge and understanding of the theatre which was quite astonishing.*
>
> Interview with the author, *Chichester Observer*, 2003

Chichester Festival
Theatre artistic directors

Sir Laurence Olivier (1962–1965)

Sir John Clements (1966–1973)

Keith Michell (1974–1977)

Peter Dews (1978–1980)

Patrick Garland (1981–1984)

John Gale (1985–1989)

Michael Rudman (1990)

Patrick Garland (1991–1994)

Sir Derek Jacobi and
Duncan C. Weldon (1995–1997)

Andrew Welch (1998–2002)

Martin Duncan, Ruth Mackenzie
and Steven Pimlott (2003–2005)

Jonathan Church (2006 to date)

With Laurence Olivier as its first artistic director, the new theatre held all the aces. Pieter Rogers, CFT general manager, in a letter to Olivier in January 1964:

*It is so vital that you appear in as many
performances of* Othello *as you can...
from the box office angle alone, we know
that when you appear in a classic, we
are virtually sold out before we start.*

THE LAURENCE OLIVIER ARCHIVE,
BRITISH MUSEUM

Evershed-Martin in a letter to Olivier:

*I doubt whether you can possibly realise
how much your actual presence during
the last two seasons in Chichester has
created a feeling of trust and confidence
in everybody that Chichester was of
importance in the theatrical world.*

IBID.

Laurence Olivier was the man whose glamour
ensured the new theatre's success. He inspired huge
loyalty in the actors who worked with him in those
early years.

Timothy Bateson on Olivier:

*We were all besotted with the man. He was
so electrifying to work with. I think he had
an understanding of the power and the
importance of acting above everything else in
the theatre. It's not to do with getting inside
the skin. It's to do with acting. He got rid of the
false and the phoney, and he was a great, great
actor. I would do anything he said.*

INTERVIEW WITH THE AUTHOR,
CHICHESTER OBSERVER, 6 AUGUST 1998

Polly Adams on Olivier:

*Sir Laurence was leading the company. I
suppose I took it for granted that it would
be a success. He was so generous to all of us.
We felt like we were his children. We even
called him 'dad' – though not to his face
because he was formidable as well. One felt
a bit paralysed when he came to give notes.
You would say to your friends afterwards
'What did he say? I didn't take it all in!'*

INTERVIEW WITH THE AUTHOR,
CHICHESTER OBSERVER, 21 JUNE 2001

Frank Finlay on Olivier:

I worked with him over many many years. We did a lot of plays together and we worked on television. I was devoted to him both as a man and as an actor.

INTERVIEW WITH THE AUTHOR, *CHICHESTER OBSERVER*, 19 SEPTEMBER 1996

Michael Elphick on Olivier:

He was a very approachable man. He had absolutely no airs or graces. I asked him several times what to do to get into acting and he said get some audition speeches together. He gave me three speeches to learn – Bottom from A Midsummer Night's Dream, *the opening speech from* Under Milk Wood *and John Osborne's* Epitaph for George Dillon.

INTERVIEW WITH THE AUTHOR, *CHICHESTER OBSERVER*, 25 FEBRUARY 1999

In the **Doctor Who** novel *The Suns of Caresh* by Paul Saint, the TARDIS crash-lands in Northgate car park near Chichester Festival Theatre – a structure the Doctor recognises and obviously likes. He points out the Festival Theatre to his assistant Jo as 'that rather splendid building' and comments that he keeps meaning to attend the opening night of Peter Shaffer's *The Royal Hunt of the Sun*: 'But I always seem to overshoot one way or another.' Also referenced in the book are: St Richard's Hospital; Graylingwell Hospital; South Street; North Street; College Lane; Bishop Otter College – and a bench (sat on by Jo) outside W. H. Smith.

CHICHESTER TIMES

Fire, Floods But No Pestilence Yet…

Thankfully, natural disaster has never turned up on Chichester's doorstep, but the city is certainly no stranger to moments of peril…

First the fires…

It was the day fire threatened to engulf Chichester's historic heart – the day a piece of Chichester's shopping heritage disappeared forever.

Shirley's, a department store selling a range of linen and clothing in North Street, was wrecked in 1974 by a night-time blaze, right in the city centre. A wind from the south-west raised fears for neighbouring buildings, and just yards away, The Dolphin & Anchor hotel was evacuated. Around sixty guests, some still in their night clothes, were led to the safety of the street. The Newell Centre, a quarter of a mile away in St Pancras, became a centre for many families and their pets forced out of their homes.

A hundred and twenty firemen from West Sussex and Hampshire in twenty-five fire engines fought the flames, but when they tried to enter the shop, they were beaten back. The blaze destroyed the shop's Georgian facade and parts of the building going back to the fourteenth century. All three storeys were left a blackened shell destined for demolition.

For nineteen years, the destruction of Shirley's remained Chichester's worst post-war blaze, until fire engulfed the **Sainsbury's** superstore on the eastern edge of the city. The company had been proud of its Chichester store, with its stylish and elegant design. But it was a design they were never to use again after fire swept through the roof one December evening in 1993. Remarkably, none of the thousand or so shoppers or staff inside the eight-year-old building was injured. The busy A27, which passes behind the building, was closed for more than three hours as thick, black smoke engulfed both carriageways. Meanwhile, more than two hundred firefighters from Sussex and Hampshire battled for more than eight hours to bring the blaze under control. By the morning, the building was a smouldering wreck.

It was the worst possible timing for the *Chichester Observer*, which had been published that morning. Senior editorial staff toyed briefly with the idea of a special Friday edition to cover Thursday's fire. Instead, they opted for ten pages of pictures and stories the following week.

The day of the fire was the chief reporter's day off. He was gutted to miss it. But not as gutted as the store was. But for scores of shoppers, Christmas had come early. The fire took place in the era of cheques, and those lucky enough to have paid for their Christmas shopping by cheque that day suddenly discovered it was theirs for free. No trace of their transaction survived the inferno.

… and then the floods

The sights were truly surreal. A lifeboat was moored to the craft shop and tearooms in the downland village of Singleton, seven miles north of Chichester; elsewhere, just to the east of the city centre, the army constructed a portable, prefabricated, World War Two-style Bailey bridge over a roundabout which sat desert-island-like in a sea of water. Nearby, people windsurfed on the river which temporarily replaced the A27 dual carriageway.

It rained and it rained, and then it rained some more. Chichester couldn't take it; the River Lavant couldn't take it; and suddenly the city and surrounding villages fell victim to the worst flooding for more than a century. After the Sainsbury's fire of December 1993, the flooding of January 1994 left the good citizens of Chichester wondering 'What next? Locusts?'

There had been nothing comparable in living memory. East of the city centre, cellars were flooded; thousands of pounds worth of stock was wrecked in dozens of shops, particularly in The Hornet; and canteens worked round the clock to feed and water the rescuers – volunteers, firefighters, soldiers, whoever was to hand – as they fought every hour of the day to second-guess the rising tide and beat it back. Local authorities went into full-scale emergency mode while the rest of the country watched aghast. Many in the city resented the national attention which created the false impression that Chichester was effectively shut; in fact, the city centre largely escaped, and Cicestrians were proud of their carry-on mentality.

Ironically, there are years when the River Lavant doesn't flow through the city at all; at the very least, it is generally dry between April and December. But in the early days of 1994, it gushed with a vengeance. The little river that at times barely trickled became a raging torrent threatening all before it. Sandbags became a feature of the city; channels were dug in a forlorn attempt to divert the flow; and slowly the arguments started. Some people contended that years of building on the flood plain had given the water nowhere to go in its moment of excess. Others argued that it was simply an act of God and that all Chichester could do was hold tight and wait. In the end, the waters eventually receded, and a massive clean-up operation – destined to last months – got under way. Flood relief schemes were put into effect, and while the Lavant flooded again during the winter of 2000–2001, it was nothing compared to the grim days of January 1994. It was officially the worst flooding for 107 years.

It has been just flood, flood, flood. Bosham, Wittering, just about everyone has been affected. It has been the whole of the county.
FIRE BRIGADE SPOKESMAN

Out of the blue a torrent of water came rushing in.
SINGLETON LANDLADY RUTH O'CONNELL

Water is coming up through the floor. We have run out of sandbags.
FARMER GARY SCOTT

Before I knew where I was, the car was up to the headlights in water. I didn't know what to do. My instinct was to put my foot down and go through it. But in fact the problem was solved for me when the engine cut out.

TRICIA GICK, OF BOSHAM HOE

It was really a case of in at the deep end. In the last week, we have served around a thousand hot meals a day.

STEVE LAWLOR, CATERING MANAGER AT COUNTY HALL

The cause is exceptionally atrocious weather conditions, a very wet autumn culminating in a deluge just after Christmas. We have already had double the average rainfall for January at this stage, and we are only halfway through the month.

TERESA CASH, NATIONAL RIVERS AUTHORITY SPOKESWOMAN

ALL FROM THE *CHICHESTER OBSERVER*, JANUARY 1994

Ghosts

Just as you would expect, Chichester, with all its rich history, is a city steeped in tales of ghosts, ghouls and things that go bump in the night. However, the staff of the *Chichester Observer* like to think that theirs is the city's most haunted building.

Unicorn House (the home of the *Chichester Observer*, on Eastgate Square) was once the Unicorn Inn, wartime haunt of many of the RAF pilots serving nearby at Tangmere – and seemingly still their haunt now. The logic goes that if you are going to come back at all, then the pub where you downed your last pint seems as good a place as any. But also in touch with the present is a pub landlord from the 1920s with a twinkle in his eye and a dodgy secret (which allegedly had something to do with stashed guns in the cellar). He manifested himself when a medium visited the building in 1994.

More sinisterly, the newspaper's staff report hearing a child crying by the stairs from time to time. A chill occasionally descends on the area occupied by the photographers, drawers inexplicably open and papers mysteriously move. It takes a strong nerve – or complete indifference – to be the last person in Unicorn House late at night.

Or indeed the first person early in the morning. I had always dismissed all the talk of ghosts in the office until one morning, alone in the newsroom in September 2012, I heard a woman's voice clearly ask 'What are you doing?' I looked around; the room was empty; I felt coldness at the back of my head; and I didn't dare move as the coldness travelled down my back. A wave of sadness without reason swept over me.

There are also tales of ghosts at **Chichester Marina** where a low humming sound has been heard, accompanied by an icy drop in temperature. An apparition in a long white gown with blonde hair has been spotted by yachtsmen and passing walkers.

The **Indian restaurant** which occupied the first floor above the disused swimming pool in Eastgate Square was also home to some strange goings-on. More than once a light source was seen to flit around the dining area. The building was demolished a few years ago, as part of the area's redevelopment, and since then the ghosts have remained invisible.

Many Chichester pubs can boast sightings of spirits other than the alcoholic kind. For many this is a badge of pride. **The Fountain**, one of the oldest public houses in Chichester, on Southgate, doesn't miss out. A man with a dog and a Roman soldier are among the unexplained visitors that have been spotted in different parts of the building over the years.

Chichester's former asylum at **Graylingwell** is one of the more obvious places to go ghost-hunting. Tales are legion of a monk who walks the grounds sandal-footed.

Racton Monument, a ruined tower built on a small hill near Funtington, five miles west of Chichester, is another place with ghostly tales to tell. Immersed in tales of smuggling, the tower is rich in atmosphere; bricks have mysteriously been thrown from the top; and a spooky woman is said to walk at night.

Chichester Traditions

Leslie Evershed-Martin gave Chichester its Festival Theatre; just a few years earlier, he also gave the city its **gala**. Mayor of Chichester at the time, Evershed-Martin conceived the event as a big day out for the family. First held in 1955, it lived up to his hopes, attracting big crowds, attractive floats and marching bands. It was organised by Chichester Combined Charities, and it had the cornflower as its emblem. Sadly, the event faded away in the 1990s and various attempts to revive it came to little, though the tide seems to have turned now. Tying in with the Queen's Diamond Jubilee, the Chichester Gala on 2 June 2012 was hailed a resounding success. The crowds were full of praise for the hard work and organisation that lay behind it, and glorious sunshine was the icing on the cake on a triumphant day for the city.

With its rich trading history, markets and fairs were important events in Chichester from the twelfth century. In about 1107–1108, Henry I granted Ralph, Bishop of Chichester, the right to hold a fair in the city – the earliest record we have of any such activity. The event became known as the **Sloe Fair** from a sloe tree in the field near the North Gate where it was held. The Sloe Fair continues to the present day in what is now the Northgate car park. Inevitably, the form of the fair has changed down the centuries: these days it is a funfair, which takes place every October.

For more than half a century, Chichester has flown the flag for the *entente cordiale* through its highly successful twinning with the French city of **Chartres**. In 1958, the Mayor and Mayoress of Chichester, Charles and Marjorie Newell, visited Chartres to help set up *le jumelage*. Representatives of the two cities agreed to unite formally in February 1959. The cities had much in common: both are located in rich farming belts, both are a similar distance from their capital, and both are home to fine cathedrals.

In 2009, the twinning's fiftieth anniversary was simultaneously celebrated on both sides of the Channel. **Ravenna** in Italy has also been twinned with Chartres, since 1957; in 1996, the circle was completed when Chichester officially twinned with Chartres's Italian twin. As with Chartres, the friendship operates through a programme of cultural and sporting exchanges.

The most arduous of Chichester's traditions was the annual **Royal Military Police (RMP) & City of Chichester International March**, which was launched in 1977. Comprising a trek up to the Downs and back, it aimed to encourage physical well-being and also to maintain a spirit of international friendship and goodwill. At its peak, marchers, both military and civilian from the UK, Europe, Canada, the USA and the Gulf States, tackled distances of 10, 25 or 40 km. With the withdrawal of the RMP from Chichester, the event lapsed in 1993, but it was relaunched by the

Rotary Club of Chichester Priory in 1998 as the
Chichester Challenge.

The most colourful of Chichester's traditions is the
festive fun had every year by the city's **Wheelbarrow
Club**, recognised as the oldest dining club in Britain.
Each year, just before Christmas, the members of the
club emerge from The Nags Head in Eastgate Square

to bestow gifts on their chosen cause, the Old Dears' Trust which provides sheltered accommodation for the elderly in Chichester. The pre-Christmas procession sees the Mayor of Chichester transported in a barrow. The tradition of wheelbarrow-carrying is believed to date back to a time when apprentices would wait outside the old Unicorn Inn to carry their drunken masters home. The club's official title is the Corporation of St Pancras. It traces its roots back to the late 1680s when it formed in support of William of Orange at the Unicorn Inn, now home to the *Chichester Observer*.

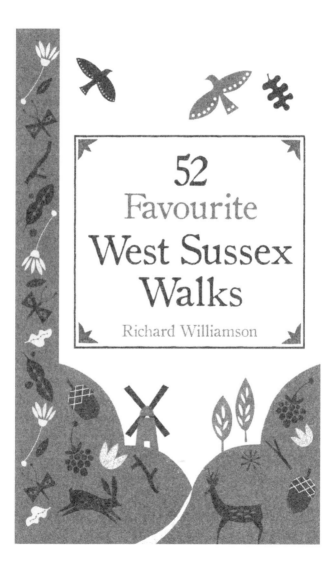

52
Favourite
West Sussex
Walks

Richard Williamson

52 FAVOURITE WEST SUSSEX WALKS

Richard Williamson

ISBN: 978 1 84953 233 4   Hardback   £9.99

Richard Williamson's weekly walking column has long been one of the most popular features in the *Chichester Observer* and *West Sussex Gazette*. Here he provides a unique insight into the West Sussex countryside with his favourite walks – one for every week of the year – with hand-drawn maps and practical notes on routes that can be covered easily in an afternoon.

Richard Williamson was for 30 years the manager of Kingley Vale National Nature Reserve and has an unparalleled knowledge of South Downs wildlife and lore.

THE
BRITISH
ISLES

A TRIVIA
GAZETTEER

PAUL ANTHONY JONES

THE BRITISH ISLES
A Trivia Gazetteer

Paul Anthony Jones

ISBN: 978 1 84953 322 5   Hardback   £12.99

DID YOU KNOW...

… that the oldest tree in Wales is a
yew in Llangernyw in Conwy, thought
to be around 4,000 years old?

… that London is one of only three
cities worldwide to have hosted both the
Olympic and Commonwealth Games?

From a Scottish waterfall three times the height of
Niagara Falls to the last foreign invasion of Britain
and the birthplace of the first Oscar-winning
Welshman, *The British Isles: A Trivia Gazetteer*
brings together hundreds of remarkable facts and
feats each pertaining to a different location in Britain
and Ireland. As much an accessible and informative
reference book as it is an entertaining miscellany, it
aims to expand our knowledge of these extraordinary
islands while uncovering and celebrating some of
their most remarkable people and places.

Have you enjoyed this book?
If so, why not write a review on
your favourite website?

If you're interested in finding out more
about our books, find us on Facebook
at **Summersdale Publishers** and follow
us on Twitter at **@Summersdale**.

Thanks very much for buying
this Summersdale book.

www.summersdale.com